Tri't
Grammar | Grammar of Biblical Aramaic   OTA = Old Tgt. Aram

of Onkelos Aramaic   OJ = Onkelos & (Torah)
＋
Jonathan (prophets)

of Palestinian Aramaic   PTM.

→ Palest. Talmud,
midrash

c̄ out distinguishing
between North ＋
South Palest. dialects,
but corresponds rather
to North (i.e. the
grammar does).

Onkelos -- text = Palestinian; & for the
most part written there (_opinion be Déaut_)
but taken to Babylon (c̄ out 5th cent.
vocalization). In Babylon, it was
vocalized (super linear); when later
transferred to Palestine (once again)
the vocalization was transferred below
the line (massoretic vocalization) –
a monstrous work, because
Aramaic was no longer spoken
in Palestine. Result – Targum
Onkelos Aramaic has no corresponding spoken language (no vocalization).

Grammar of
PALESTINIAN JEWISH
ARAMAIC

BY

Wm. B. STEVENSON, D.Litt

SECOND EDITION

WITH AN

APPENDIX ON THE NUMERALS

BY

J. A. EMERTON

OXFORD
AT THE CLARENDON PRESS

Oxford University Press, Ely House, London W. 1

GLASGOW NEW YORK TORONTO MELBOURNE WELLINGTON
CAPE TOWN SALISBURY IBADAN NAIROBI LUSAKA ADDIS ABABA
BOMBAY CALCUTTA MADRAS KARACHI LAHORE DACCA
KUALA LUMPUR HONG KONG

FIRST EDITION 1924
REPRINTED LITHOGRAPHICALLY IN GREAT BRITAIN
AT THE UNIVERSITY PRESS, OXFORD
FROM SHEETS OF THE FIRST EDITION
1950, 1956
SECOND EDITION 1962
REPRINTED 1966

NOTE ON THE SECOND EDITION

In this second edition Dr. Stevenson's text remains unchanged, but it has been thought right to repair a long-standing omission by the addition of an Appendix on the Numerals, which has kindly been supplied by the Rev. J. A. Emerton, Lecturer in Divinity in the University of Cambridge.

PREFACE TO THE FIRST EDITION

THIS introduction to Palestinian Jewish Aramaic presupposes a general knowledge of Hebrew or of some other Semitic language, such as Syriac or Arabic. It is intended primarily to equip students for the reading of the Targums (OJ) and the Aramaic portions of the Palestinian Talmud and Midrashim (PTM), and to provide a help to the study of the Aramaic elements contained in the writings of the New Testament.

The Aramaic of the books of Ezra and Daniel is perhaps best learned after a study has been made of one of the dialects just named. Its forms and uses, therefore, are noted in a supplementary way throughout the grammar. At the same time those who choose to begin with Old Testament Aramaic (OTA) may do so with the help of the special paradigms at the end of the book and by concentrating chiefly on the notes marked OTA, which have been placed towards the close of most of the sections into which the grammar is divided.

The pioneer work of Gustaf Dalman is everywhere presupposed and made use of. His grammar of OJ and PTM formulates the now accepted principles of their treatment (see p. 9) and provides an inexhaustible store-house of material for further investigation. In accordance with his conclusions the punctuation of the supralinear MSS. is taken as a standard, although transliterated uniformly into the familiar sublinear system and so, in some particulars, made more precise (see § 2).

Dalman's grammar does not include syntax, so that the notes on syntax are a special feature of this grammar and are based almost entirely on the writer's personal observations. The references added to the syntactical notes, and in other cases also, are intended to show the range of the evidence found, and to make it easy to test and supplement the conclusions drawn. They are not intended to be used by beginners. The evidence for the syntax of PTM has been taken wholly from the texts of Dalman's *Dialektproben*.

The scantiness of the material available for the study of OTA often makes the formulation of general statements about it difficult and practically inexpedient. The method adopted, therefore, has frequently been that of giving a precise numerical statement of the facts. The paradigm of the verb, also, has been made, more closely than is usual, a reproduction of existing verbal forms. Strack's edition of the texts, in his *Biblical Aramaic Grammar*, is assumed to be referred to, except when otherwise stated. Special note has been made of the evidence of the supralinear MSS. of OTA, of which Strack gives specimens.

References to the Targum of Onkelos are made implicitly to the supralinear editions of Kahle, Merx, and Praetorius, so far as they go (see Literature, p. 8). In the case of Gen. 1–4 and 24, the source is Merx's *Chrestomathy*, for other parts of the Pentateuch, Berliner's *Onkelos* is used. The references to Dalman's *Dialektproben* are made by means of figures referring to the page, paragraph, and line, generally without mention of the title, sometimes with the abbreviation Chrest. prefixed.

Much of the material in most sections of the grammar may be passed over on a first reading. Students working without a teacher are recommended to confine themselves at first to the notes marked with an asterisk. One or two sections which should be read completely are similarly marked. Those who have a fair working knowledge of Hebrew may begin to read the chapters of Genesis contained in Merx's *Chrestomathy* after they have completed § 8 of the *Grammar*. Only texts with a supralinear vocalization should be used at first. Dalman's interesting *Dialektproben*, if it can be obtained, may be commenced at p. 14, after a few chapters of the Targum have been read. Unfortunately the *Dialektproben* is now out of print and there is no immediate prospect of its re-issue. The publication of further selections from the Aramaic portions of the Jerusalem Talmud, with an English vocabulary, would be of great assistance to English students of this literature.

The language of the *Aramaic Papyri of the Fifth Century B.C.*, recently edited and translated by A. Cowley (1923), is closely related to the idioms of OJ, PTM, and OTA. The announcement by the editor of his intention to publish a grammar of the dialect of these papyri makes it superfluous to apologize for its exclusion from the scope of the present work. Still it may be said that, on the scale of treatment here attempted, no more than three dialects could properly be included. A more comprehensive work must be preceded by other detailed studies, which do not yet exist.

It is a very pleasant duty to acknowledge the help and encouragement the writer has received from the members of the *Society for Old Testament Study*, both individually and collectively. Without the assurance of their support and interest this grammar would never have been published nor expanded into its present form. Special thanks are due to my friend, the energetic and resourceful secretary, Dr. T. H. Robinson, of Cardiff University College.

I am greatly obliged to the readers of the Clarendon Press for their vigilant attention to every detail and to the Delegates for the cordiality of their acceptance of my work. My Assistant, Mr. E. J. Harris, B.D., has twice read through the proofs and has verified many references and has helped to remove inaccuracies that might otherwise have escaped detection.

WM. B. STEVENSON

Glasgow, 5 March 1924

TABLE OF CONTENTS

		PAGE
Preface	. . . .	3
Literature	. . . .	8
1. Introduction	. . . . . .	9
2. Orthography	. . . . . .	11
3. Personal Pronouns (nominative forms)	. . .	15
4. ,, ,, (suffix forms)	. . . .	16
5. Demonstrative Pronouns and Adjectives	. .	18
6. Interrogatives	. . . . . .	20
7. The Relative Pronoun	. . . . . .	21
8. Nouns and Adjectives (general)	. . . .	22
9. Classification of Nouns (declensions)	. . .	26
10. Inflexion of Nouns (masculine types)	. . .	29
11. ,, ,, (feminines)	. . .	34
12. Pronominal Suffixes (with singular nouns)	. .	38
13. ,, ,, (with masc. plur. stems)	.	40
14. ,, ,, (with fem. plur. stems)	. .	42
15. לֵית, אִית, &c.	. . . . . .	43
16. Verbal Stems	. . . . . .	44
17. Perfect Tenses	. . . . . .	46
18. Imperfect Tenses	. . . . .	48
19. Imperatives	. . . . . .	51
20. Infinitives	. . . . . .	52
21. Participles	. . . . . .	54
22. Compound Tenses	. . . . .	57
23. Influence of Gutturals upon Verbal Forms	. .	60

PAGE

24. Verbs, initial Nun 61
25. ,,   initial Aleph 63
26. ,,   initial Yodh and Waw 65
27. ,,   final Yodh and Aleph 66
28. ,,   ,,   ,,   ,, perfect tenses . . . 68
29. ,,   ,,   ,,   ,, impff., imperatt., and infinn. 70
30. ,,   ,,   ,,   ,, inflexion of particc. . . 72
31. הֲלַךְ, חֲיָא, הֲוָה, אֲתָא 73
32. Monosyllabic Stems (ע״י) 75
33.   ,,   ,, (inflected forms) 77
34. Partially Monosyllabic Stems (ע״ע) 78
35.   :,   ,.   ,, (inflected forms) . . 80
36. Verbal Suffixes 81
37. ,,   ,, (with ל״א stems) 84
38. ,,   ,, (in OTA) 86
    Paradigm of Verb (OJ) 88
    ,,   ,, Verbal Suffixes 90
    Tables of OTA 92
    Appendix on the Numerals
       by J. A. EMERTON 97
39. Cardinal Numbers 99
40. Ordinal Numbers 104
41. Other Numerals 105

LITERATURE

BERLINER, A. Targum Onkelos (text, with introduction and notes). Berlin, 1884.

Massorah zum Targum Onkelos. Leipzig, 1877.

BURNEY, C. F. Aramaic Origin of the Fourth Gospel. Oxford, 1922.

DALMAN, GUSTAF. Grammatik des Jüdisch-Palästinischen Aramäisch. Zweite Auflage. Leipzig, 1905.

Aramäisch-Neuhebräisches Handwörterbuch zu Targum, Talmud und Midrasch. Zweite verbesserte und vermehrte Auflage. Frankfurt a. Main, 1922.

Aramäische Dialektproben... mit Wörterverzeichnis. Leipzig, 1896.

Worte Iesu. Leipzig, 1898. (English trans., T. & T. Clark, 1902.)

DIETTRICH. Grammatische Beobachtungen zu drei ... Handschriften des Onqelostargums. ZATW xx 1900 (pp. 148–59).

KAHLE, PAUL. Masoreten des Ostens—die ältesten punktierten Handschriften des Alten Testaments und der Targume (in Kittel's Beiträge, Heft 15). Leipzig, 1913.

LAGARDE, PAUL DE. Prophetae chaldaice. Leipzig, 1872.

LANDAUER, S. Studien zu Merx' Chrestomathia targumica. In Zeitschrift für Assyriologie, vol. iii, 1888 (pp. 263–92).

MERX, ADALBERT. Chrestomathia Targumica (with critical notes and Latin glossary). Berlin, 1888.

PRAETORIUS, FRANZ. Targum zu Josua in Jemenischer Überlieferung. Berlin, 1899.

Targum zum Buch der Richter in Jemenischer Überlieferung. Berlin, 1900.

STRACK, H. L. Grammatik des Biblisch-Aramäischen, mit ... Texten und einem Wörterbuch. 6te Auflage. Munich, 1921.

PALESTINIAN JEWISH ARAMAIC

§ 1. INTRODUCTION

DALMAN'S *Grammar of Jewish-Palestinian Aramaic* (Leipzig, 1894) opened a new period in the study of the Aramaic dialects. It separated clearly for the first time the dialects of the Targums, Talmuds, and Midrashim, and it supplied a coherent and correct vocalization of the grammatical forms of the Targum of Onkelos and of the related dialect used in the Palestinian Talmud. The vocalization was based upon Yemenite MSS., which employed supralinear vowel signs. The second edition of Dalman's grammar (1905), along with his dictionary (1901), supplemented and revised his early work, but did not change its fundamental character.

It was now made clear that the Targums of Onkelos (Pentateuch) and Jonathan (Prophets) were written in practically the same Aramaic dialect (OJ), somewhat modified by the influence of the Hebrew originals, and that the Palestinian Talmud and Midrashim preserved the remains of another dialect (PTM), closely related to the former. Because of this relationship Dalman supplied the unvocalized texts of PTM with vowels determined for the most part by the analogy of the supralinear tradition of the Targums. In this whole literature he saw, with good reason, the best avenue of approach to the Aramaic speech of Palestine in the time of Christ and a valuable help to the study of the language and thought of the New Testament.

The origin, character, and variations of the supralinear MSS. of the Targums have been greatly elucidated by the patient and extensive researches of Paul Kahle (published in 1913). His conclusions may be summarized as follows. The oldest and best tradition of the Aramaic of the Targums is contained in MSS. of Babylonian (i.e. Mesopotamian) origin. The Yemenite MSS. represent this tradition modified by the principles of the school of Tiberias in Palestine. The measure of Palestinian influence increased as time went on, so that the older Yemenite MSS. are nearer to the Babylonian tradition than the later. The sublinear vocalization of Berliner's edition of Onkelos goes back ultimately to a MS. which used the supralinear system. The forms of Berliner's edition are not real Aramaic forms, but through them we may reach a supralinear tradition similar to that of the MSS. which employ a supralinear vocalization.

The texts of PTM are to a large extent stories written in a simple popular style. The language, according to Dalman, is that of Galilee in the third and fourth centuries A.D. Part of what is contained in the Midrashim may be dated as late as the sixth century. There are some differences of vocabulary between the Targums of Onkelos and Jonathan, but no very obvious differences of grammar. The Aramaic of these Targums has a more literary character than the language of the Galilean stories, and is supposed to have been moulded first in Judea. The Targums themselves may not have received their final literary form before the fifth century, but the idiom in which they are written probably goes back at least to the second century and perhaps earlier. Dalman's interpretation of the phraseology of the New Testament in the light of Aramaic usage proceeds on the view that we have in OJ and PTM, respectively, close approximations to the literary and popular forms of the language of Palestine in the time of Christ.[1]

---

[1] See especially Dalman's *Words of Jesus*, Introduction, section viii. The most recent attempt to show the influence of Aramaic upon a NT writer is

§ 2.[1] ORTHOGRAPHY

1. In unvocalized texts (PTM) א, ה, ו, and י are freely used to
indicate vowels. Waw and yodh frequently denote short vowels,
as well as long vowels. Typical examples are: מִלָּה = מילה,
איתיליד = אִתֵּין = אתין, עֶנְלָא = עינלא, מְקַטַּל = מיקטל, אָנּוּן = אינן
or חָפָא, חֹפָא = חֹמָא, כַּלְיֵה = כוליה, גֻּבְרָא = גובּרא, אִתְיְלִיד = אתיליד. The
stem vowel of the inflected forms of segholate nouns (עיגלא) and
the preformative vowel of verbal reflexives (איתיליד) are commonly
indicated in this way. The insertion of vowel signs into texts originally
unvocalized accounts for the existence of forms like מִיקַטַל, אִינּוּן, &c.
In unvocalized texts וו and יי may be written for consonantal waw
and yodh in the middle of a word (e. g. לְיִלְךָ = לילון), and יי for
diphthongal *ai* or for י pronounced as a double consonant, with
daghesh (e.g. קַיָּם = קיים). א and ה both represent a final long
vowel, especially *ā*. In PTM and OJ א is the more commonly
used. In OTA א is preferred in some cases, e. g. to represent the
emphatic ending א (§ 8), ה in other cases, e. g. in the feminine
termination הֽ‍ָ. In מאן (who?) and עאל (he entered) א denotes
the short *ă*, in order to distinguish these words from the prepositions מִן and עַל. But מַן and עַל are generally used. Final diphthongal *ai* is often denoted by אי.

2. The punctuation of the MSS. of Babylonian origin published
by Kahle is by no means uniform, varying through several stages
from a quite simple system to one which is highly complex. The
system of the Yemenite MSS. is a variation of the simple Babylonian
system, and the resemblances and differences of these two are,
principally, what is explained in the following notes.

C. F. Burney's *Aramaic Origin of the Fourth Gospel* (1922). It gives a most
valuable synopsis of the Aramaic idioms and constructions which may be
looked for in the Greek of NT.

[1] This section may be omitted when the grammar is being read for the first
time. A knowledge of the ordinary Hebrew alphabet is presupposed.

3. In the simple Babylonian punctuation there are signs for daghesh (a supralinear ג or ˄) and raphe (supralinear ר or ⌒), which, however, are seldom used (Kahle, p. 167). Some Yemenite MSS. do not employ daghesh at all (as in Merx, pp. 57 ff.), others regularly use the Palestinian sign (so in Judges and Joshua as edited by Praetorius). The supralinear MSS. of OTA in Strack occasionally exhibit the Babylonian signs for daghesh (Dan. 4. 24, 5. 8, 12, &c.) and raphe (Dan. 5. 7, 12).

4. The supralinear punctuation at first had no sign equivalent to the Palestinian silent shewa. Some Babylonian MSS., however, which use a complex system of punctuation, employ the sign for vocal shewa ambiguously as in the Palestinian system. In Yemenite MSS. the shewa sign usually represents only vocal shewa, although in some few cases it may represent Palestinian silent shewa also.

5. Pathaḥ furtive is seldom represented in either the Babylonian or the Yemenite MSS., but was, presumably, pronounced in the positions indicated by the Palestinian tradition, and so may be introduced into a sublinear transliteration of the supralinear signs. The suffix ֵיהּ (§ 4) is, however, to be excepted from this treatment, in accordance with the analogy of OTA.

6. The following vowel signs are used in the supralinear system of the simplest type:

Qameṣ . .	˂	Ḥolem . . .	:
Pathaḥ and seghol	˗	Shureq . . .	ˈ
Ṣere . . .	··	Vocal shewa . . (including ḥaṭephs)	⸝
Ḥireq . .	·		

The first six of these signs denote regularly both long vowels and short vowels. Qameṣ at first had only the sound of *ā* in 'psalm' (approximately), not that of *ā* in 'ball', and ḥolem represented both Palestinian *ŏ* and Palestinian ḥolem. The later Yemenite MSS., however, use qameṣ for *ŏ*, so that, at different

periods, both בֿל and בֿכ were pronounced as Hebrew כָּל־. No
distinction is made in the representation of pathaḥ and seghol,
although, presumably, both sounds were used in actual speech. In
transliterating the supralinear pathaḥ into sublinear writing, the
analogy of OTA and of Hebrew will determine our choice between
sublinear pathaḥ and sublinear seghol.

7. In Babylonian and sporadically in Yemenite MSS., pathaḥ is
used for ḥateph pathaḥ, following א and ע and sometimes following
ה and ח (e.g. אַמַר for אֲמַר, אַעֲבֵיד for אַעֲבֵיד). This usage occurs
in the supralinear MSS. of OTA (Dan. 3. 12, 3. 13, 4. 28, 4. 29),
but not consistently (Dan. 4. 32 עֲבַדְתְּ, 5. 5 שָׁעֲתָה).

8. Some supralinear MSS. have forms like אֵירַחֵים, אִילָהָא, אֵינָשׁ
(= Hebrew אֲרַחֵם, אֱלֹהִים, אֱנֹשׁ), instead of forms commencing with
אֱ or אֲ. It is possible that this orthography represents an alternative pronunciation of the words in question, but more likely that
yodh, with ṣere, simply represented ֵ, just as pathaḥ stood for ֲ.
Similarly נֵיצַלֵּי (*Chrest.* 29. 21) was neither a phonetic variant nor
a grammatical equivalent of נְצַלֵּי (1 plur. impf. Pael), but was,
originally, precisely the same word, differently spelled. This use
of yodh (with ṣere) to denote vocal shewa occurs in the supralinear
MSS. of OTA, and it throws fresh light on the Hebrew forms
referred to in Gesenius-Kautzsch, § 23 h (אֵזוֹר = אֲזוֹר).

9. Some supralinear MSS. write ִי instead of ְ, especially at the
beginning of words, but also in other cases (e.g. in דִּיְרֵי = דְּיְרֵי,
Deut. 9. 28—Kahle, p. 14). This alternative orthography may
also be understood to imply an alternative pronunciation—*yĭ* or *ĭ*
(cf. Syriac)—but it should rather be regarded as an alternative way
of representing the sound that is usually written as vocal shewa

10. Ḥateph qameṣ is sometimes explicitly written in Yemenite
MSS., especially in those of later date and especially in certain
words, such as קֳדָם.

11. With the exceptions already noted, the ḥatephs of the sublinear system are not specially represented in the supralinear writing. Still the distinctive sounds of the ḥaṭephs were no doubt employed by those who wrote the supralinear system. The forms וּ (and) and דּ (who, which), which are used before certain consonants followed by vocal shewa, may be taken as proof that these following consonants were pronounced with ḥaṭeph pathaḥ. Ḥaṭephs may therefore be employed in transliterating the supralinear into the sublinear system.

12. In Babylonian MSS. and in the supralinear MSS. of OTA (Strack) וּ is the form of the conjunction 'and' before words commencing with a consonant followed by vocal shewa (Dan. 3. 21, 4. 29, 5. 20, 6. 5, 6. 17), even when that following consonant is בּ, מ, or פ (Dan. 5. 11, 6. 11). Before בּ, מ, and פ not followed by vocal shewa, the form of the conjunction is וּ, implicitly, at least, since the vowel is generally not explicitly represented. In the Yemenite MSS. of OJ וּ is used in all these cases, as in sublinear Hebrew texts (so in Praetorius's edition of Joshua and Judges and in Berliner's *Onkelos*).

13. When the initial consonant of a word is followed by vocal shewa simple, the supralinear punctuation does not indicate its presence if it is preceded by the conjunction וּ or וּ (Gen. 1. 10, 1. 17, Judg. 1. 17, 1. 22, Dan. 3. 21, 5. 11, 6. 17, &c.). This may imply that the vocal shewa in these cases, as in Hebrew לְקְטֹל and וְהָיוּ, was no longer pronounced (so Dalman, p. 240). Some MSS. treat words that commence with ה and ח in the same way so that, for example, וַחֲזָא may perhaps be an alternative for וַחֲזָא (cf. Heb. לַחְפֹּר).

In the Babylonian MSS. and in the supralinear MSS. of OTA (Strack), however, vocal shewa following an initial consonant is frequently unrepresented in writing, especially in association with particular forms or words, such as the particles בּ, כּ, לּ, and וּ. This implies that the absence of the sign of a hurried vowel (vocal shewa) is not a certain proof of its absence in speech, and makes any conclusion regarding the case of the preceding paragraph uncertain.

14. In OTA the diphthong *ai* causes mutation, like a simple vowel, and silent shewa is written after the yodh of the diphthong (e.g. in הָיִיתִי, הֲוֵיתָ, בֵּיתֵהּ). Compare also, perhaps, קַרְמָיְתָא (§ 11, note 12) and מְנוּחָיְכִי (Ps. 116. 7, in the Hebrew Psalter). These analogies may be allowed to determine the sublinear vocalization of OJ and PTM in such words as הַיְדֵין (§ 6), עֶבְדָיְתָא (§ 11, note 7), אַיְתִי (§ 31), and the pronominal suffixes ‑ַיְכִי and ‑ַיְהָא (§ 13).

§ 3. PERSONAL PRONOUNS (nominative forms)

	PTM		OJ		
PLUR.	SING.	PLUR.	SING.		
אֲנַן	אֲנָא	אֲנַחְנָא (נַחְנָא)	אֲנָא	1 com.
אַתּוּן	אַתְּ (אַנְתְּ)	אַתּוּן	אַתְּ	2 masc.
—	אַתְּ (אַנְתְּ)	אַתֵּין	אַתְּ	fem.
אינון, הינון	הוּא	אִנּוּן	הוּא	3 masc.
אינין, הינין	הִיא	אִנֵּין	הִיא	fem.

Accent. **1*.** In OJ and OTA the pronouns of the 1 person plural are accented on the penultimate syllable. This is one of the few exceptions to the general rule in these dialects that the last syllable of a word is accented.

Forms. **2.** The shortened forms נָא, נַן, and תּוּן sometimes occur independently in PTM (cf. נָשׁ for אֱנָשׁ and נַחְנָא for אֲנַחְנָא). They, and אַתְּ = תְּ, also coalesce with participles into tense forms (§ 21, note 7).

3*. אינון, &c., are unvocalized spellings equivalent to אִנּוּן, &c. (§ 2. 1).

OTA. **4.** For the forms of OTA see paradigm, p. 92. The last letter of אֲנַחְנָא is א three times and once ה. אנתה is a Kᵉthibh form, always changed to אַנְתְּ by Qᵉre, but pointed אַנְתָּה by the supralinear MSS. in Strack. אַנּוּן and הִמּוֹ occur, as nominatives, each once only.

Idioms. **5.** The expressions הַהוּא גֻּבְרָא ('a certain man', § 5, note 12) and הָהִיא אִתְּתָא are used by PTM in modesty for אֲנָא (cf. Hebrew עַבְדְּךָ) and in curses or protestations for אַתְּ. In polite address, for אַתְּ, OJ uses רִבּוֹנִי and רִבּוֹנִי and PTM מָרָן, מָרִי, רַבִּי and רַבָּנָן (cf. Hebrew אֲדֹנִי).

6. For 'he himself', &c., see § 4, note 6.

§ 4. PERSONAL PRONOUNS (suffix forms)

PTM	OJ	OJ, PTM	
PLUR.	PLUR.	SING.	
ָ ן	נָא ¹	ִ י	1 com.
כוֹן	כוֹן	ָ ךְ	2 masc.
כֵין	כֵין	יךְ	fem.
הוֹן , וֹן	הוֹן	יה	3 masc.
הֵין	הֵין	ה	fem.

1*. These suffixes are equivalent to English possessive adjectives and to the genitives of the personal pronouns in other languages. For the possessive pronouns see § 7, note 4.

Forms. **2.** The suffixes of the table are those joined to the singular stems of nouns ending with a consonant. In slightly different forms they are attached to verbs to express the accusatives of the personal pronouns (§ 36). יכִי (2 s. f.) and הָא (3 s. f.), used in the marriage contract printed in Dalman's *Dialektproben*, p. 4 (ll. 4, 5, 6, 8), are older, uncontracted, forms of יךְ and ה respectively. See also § 12, note 2, and § 13. For the variations of OTA, see p. 93.

---

¹ See § 3, note 1.

3. Merx (*Chrest. Targum.*) prints קִבְלָא in Gen. 2. 20 for קָבְלֵיהּ and תְּחוֹתָא for תְּחוֹתֵהּ in Gen. 2. 21.

Accus. Cases. **4*.** The accusatives of the personal pronouns are expressed in three ways: (1) by suffixes (§ 36), (2) by יָתִי, &c., (3) by לִי, &c. OJ nearly always follows the Hebrew text in its choice between a verbal suffix and an independent accusative form. In the latter case it regularly employs יתי, &c., seldom לי, &c. For לֵיהּ and לְהוֹן after particc. see Gen. 3. 15 and Exod. 3. 9.

In PTM לי, &c., are used as accusatives after participles (18. 12, 19. 5, 20. 11, 14, &c.) and sometimes after finite forms of the verb (16. ii. 9, 26. 3, 28. 15). A pronominal object after a verb is usually expressed by a suffix. יתי, &c., occur after participles (16. ii. 3, 23. 2), perfects (19. ii. 14, 21. 7, 25. ii. 5), and impff. (22. ii. 5).

In OTA the pronominal object of a verb is generally expressed by means of a suffix. But only the independent forms הִמּוֹ (in Ezra), הִמּוֹן (in Daniel) and אִנּוּן (Dan. 6. 25) are used for 'them'. יָת with a suffix occurs once (Dan. 3. 12, וְיָתְהוֹן), לי, &c., only with participles (Dan. 2. 23, 4. 22, 29, 6. 17, Ezra 5. 2).

Ethic Dative. **5.** לִי, &c., are also used as 'ethic datives', especially after verbs of motion. Examples: נְפַק לֵיהּ (26. 5), מְדַפְּקָא לַהּ (24. ii. 5).

Reflex. Pron. **6*.** In PTM the reflexive pronouns are generally expressed by גַּרְמִי, &c., sometimes by נַפְשִׁי, &c. (Dalman, p. 115, § 13). In OJ the pronominal suffixes are used, in agreement with the Hebrew text, נפשי, &c., being occasional alternatives. In PTM emphatic 'he himself' is expressed by כֹּל גַּרְמֵיהּ, 'this itself' by כֹּל גַּרְמָא דָא (דָא = this, § 5). גַּרְמִי means, literally, 'my bone' (for its inflexion see § 12, note 4).

OTA. **7.** In MT נָא (Baer, Ginsburg) is usual for נָ־, but cf. pausal שֵׁיזְבוּתַנָא (Dan. 3. 17). כֹם and הֹם occur only in Ezra, as alternatives to כוֹן and הוֹן. See Brockelmann, *Grundriss*, I. 113.

§ 5. DEMONSTRATIVE PRONOUNS AND ADJECTIVES

	PTM	PTM	OJ	OJ
	ADJECTIVES.	PRONOUNS.	ADJECTIVES.	PRONOUNS.
this	הָדֵין, הָדָא, הָדֵין, הָא	דֵין, דְּנָא	הָדֵין	דֵין (דְּנָא)
	הָרָא	דָא	הָדָא	דָא
these	הָלֵין	אִלֵּין, אִילִין	הָאִלֵּין	אִלֵּין

ADJECTIVES AND PRONOUNS.

	PTM	PTM	OJ	OJ
that	הַהוּא	הָדָךְ, הָךְ	הָהוּא (דֵּיכִי)	דֵּיכִי
	הָהִיא, הָאִי, הָיי	הָךְ	הָהִיא	דָּךְ
those	היינון, אינון	—	הָאִנּוּן	אִלֵּיךְ

Forms. **1*.** הָהוּא and הָהִיא are the forms of the Babylonian MSS. published by Kahle. הַהוּא and הַהִיא in the supralinear Yemenite MSS. are Hebraisms (Dalman). הָלֵין (16. ii. 7) is pointed הָלֵין in Dalman's paradigm (p. 397).

2*. אִילִין, היינון, and אינם are the unvocalized spellings of PTM (§ 2. 1).

3. הֵידֵין, הֵידָא, and הֵילֵין occur as alternatives to הָדֵין, &c. (e. g. 15. 6) and are cited by Dalman (p. 111), but are held by him to be incorrect forms (p. 120).

4. PTM has a number of forms such as אָהֵין and אָהָן (28. 24) in which א alternates with ה. It also frequently uses contracted forms (הָלֵין, הָאִי, &c.). דֵּין and הָדֵין coalesce with a following הוּא into דֵּינוּ and הֵינוּ. ל, כ, ו join with הָאִי into לְיי, כָּיי, וָיי (Dalman, p. 112).

OTA. **5.** For OTA forms see paradigm (p. 92). אֵנּוּן for ' those ' (Dan. 2. 44) and אֵלֶּה for ' these ' (Ezra 5. 15) occur each once only. דִּכֵּן ' that ' is both masculine (once) and feminine (twice). In OTA the same forms are used, without distinction, as adjectives and pronouns. See also notes 10 and 14.

Special usages. **6.** דְּנַן occurs in PTM as an enclitic particle following interrogative pronouns (Dalman, *Grammar*, pp. 111 and 224). In OJ it is similarly used to translate זֶה after לָמָּה (Gen. 25. 22) and also for זֶה associated with a numeral (Gen. 27. 36, Judg. 16. 15). כִּדְנָן is sometimes used by OJ as a translation of Hebrew כֹּה (Gen. 45. 9, Exod. 3. 14 f., 5. 10, 7. 26, Josh. 24. 2, Judg. 11. 15, 2 Kings 19. 20).

7*. דֵּיכִי is usually equivalent to הַלָּזֶה (Judg. 6. 20, &c.) and seldom occurs otherwise (Gen. 27. 33). The pronoun 'that' in OJ is also expressed by הוּא (Gen. 2. 19, 41. 28, 42. 14, Exod. 16. 23, Amos 7. 6), which might, therefore, properly be included in the table.

Syntax. **8*.** OJ generally distinguishes between adjective and pronoun forms. Exceptions are: (*a*) דֵּיכִי, (*b*) דֵּין instead of הָדֵין, after a noun with a pronominal suffix attached, under the influence of the Hebrew text (Exod. 10. 1, Josh. 2. 20, Judg. 6. 14), (*c*) the phrase הַיּוֹם = יוֹמָא דֵין 'to-day' (cf. יוֹמָא הָדֵין 'this day'), (*d*) כְּהָדָא (Judg. 13. 23, 15. 7).

9. In PTM הָהוּא generally serves as the pronoun 'that' (16. ii. 11 and 13, 18. ii. 3) and other singular adjective forms are also freely used as pronouns (15. 6, 16. ii. 12, 28. 24).

On the other hand, pronoun forms are used as adjectives (18. ii. 10 and 11—דֵּין, 28. 13—אִנּוּן). אִלֵּין, in particular, occurs more often than הָלֵּין as an adjective (16. ii. 10, 17. ii. 8, 20. 21, 24. ii. 1).

10*. In PTM a demonstrative nearly always stands before its associated noun (two exceptions in *Chrest.* 20. 12 and 21. 15 are both from the same narrative). In OJ the influence of the Hebrew text has established the rule that demonstratives follow the nouns they qualify. Exceptions agree with the order of the Hebrew text (Gen. 2. 23, Judg. 16. 15, &c.) In OTA a demonstrative adjective generally follows, but may precede, an associated noun (Dan. 2. 44).

11. Nouns qualified by a demons. adjective nearly always assume the emphatic form (see § 8, note 3).

Idioms. **12.** הָדֵין is used with proper names in the sense of 'the well-known' or 'the previously-mentioned' (15. ii. 2, 17. ii. 1; similarly 22. ii. 9). הַהוּא is sometimes equivalent to פְּלָנִי 'a certain', e.g. in the phrases גַּבְרָא הַהוּא, הַהוּא יוֹמָא. דֵּין . . . דֵּין (and חַר . . . חַר) express 'this . . . that' or 'one . . . another'.

13. יָת with suffixes of the third person is sometimes used as a demons. adjective or pronoun, like אֹתוֹ, &c., in the Mishnah (Dalman, § 17. 8).

14. In OTA before a noun governed by a preposition an anticipative pronominal suffix is used in an emphasizing demonstrative sense (בֵּהּ זִמְנָא 'at that very time'). The noun is then in the emphatic form (§ 8). So in PTM אֲמַר לֵיהּ לְרַבָּן יוֹחָנָן 'he said to this same R. Jochanan' (20. ii. 10).

§ 6. INTERROGATIVES

	PTM	OJ	
who?	מַן, מָאן	מַן	
what?	מָה	מָא	
which?	היידין	אֵידֵין	sing. masc.
,,	היידא, אֵידא	אֵידָא	fem.
,,	היילין, אֵילין	(אִילֵין)	plural com.

Forms. **1*.** For the spelling מָאן see § 2. 1. אִילֵין happens not to occur in OJ. היידין, &c., are the unvocalized spellings of הָאֵידֵין, &c. (§ 2. 1 and 14).

2. In PTM מַן הוּא contracts into מַנּוּ and מָא הִיא into מָי. In OJ מָא דֵּין = מָדֵין (note 4).

Usages. **3*.** The meanings of מָא are: what? how? what kind of? and (with adjectives) how! מָא לְ (לְמָה) expresses 'why?' and

כְּמָא (כְּמָה) 'how many?' Questions introduced by לְמָא so often expect a negative answer that this interrogative acquires the sense of a negative (§ 7, note 7).

4. In OJ מָא דֵין or מָדֵין renders Hebrew מַה־זֶּה (Gen. 27. 20, Judg. 18. 24), but לְמָא דְנָן is used for לָמָה־זֶּה (§ 5, note 6).

Syntax. 5. אִידִין, &c., are both pronouns and adjectives. Their associated nouns may stand in the emphatic form (*Chrest.* 23. 3 and 4, Isai. 66. 1), but not necessarily.

Interrog. Adverbs. 6. אָן (OJ) and הָן (PTM) = 'where?', לְאָן = 'whither?' and מָן אָן = 'whence?' מִנָּן (Gen. 29. 4) is also written for מָן אָן.

OTA. 7. Only מַן and מָה occur in OTA. Most editors, including Baer and Ginsburg, point the former מָן. In Dan. 3. 33 כְּמָה (with an adjective) = how!

§ 7. THE RELATIVE PRONOUN

Forms. 1*. In OJ and PTM the relative pronoun is דְּ (uninflected). In OTA and in OJ compounds (דִּילִי, &c., note 4) the form is דִּי.

Idioms. 2*. דְּ without an antecedent means 'that which', 'he who', 'those who', &c. מַן דְּ, הָהוּא דְּ, הָדֵין דְּ, הָרֵין דְּ, and מָא דְּ are also used to express these combinations.

3*. דְּ before a genitive means 'the possession of', 'those of', 'those belonging to', &c. E.g. דְּבֵיתִי = 'the people of my house'. In reports of the opinions of the Rabbis, before the name of a Rabbi, it stands for 'the opinion of'.

Compounds. 4*. דִּילִי, דִּילָךְ, &c., 'that which is to me', 'that which is to thee', &c., are the equivalents of the possessive pronouns mine, thine, &c., in OJ (cf. Dan. 2. 20). In PTM דִּירִי, &c., are more usual. דִּירִי may be a phonetic variant of דִּילִי (Barth) or = דְּ + יְדִי 'the possession of my hand' (Dalman).

5. לְ + דִּ + מָא, with suffixes, is treated as a substantive, meaning property (16. ii. 2, מְדִלְיַהּ).

6. In PTM דּוּ is a contraction for דְּהוּא and דִּי occurs as a contraction for דִּהִיא (Dalman, p. 98).

Conjunctional uses. **7*.** דִּ is much used as a conjunction,
—of time (when), place (where), cause (because), purpose (in order that), and introducing subject and object sentences (= Hebrew כִּי 'that'). Joined to prepositions it gives them the force of conjunctions (מִן דִּ = after, עַד דִּ = until or whilst). דִּלְמָא כַּד 'when' and 'lest' or 'perhaps' (Ezra 7. 23 דִּי לְמָה) are compounds with כְּ and לְמָא (§ 6, note 3) respectively. בְּדִיל דִּ is used for 'because' and 'in order that'.

Relative Adverbs. **8*.** The relative adverbs—where, whither, and whence—are expressed in PTM by לְהָן דִּ, הָן דִּ, מָן הָן דִּ, and (cf. § 6, note 6) and in OJ generally by דִּ . . תַּמָּן, דִּ . . לְתַמָּן, and דִּ . . מִתַּמָּן (cf. OTA דִּי . . תַּמָּה, Ezra 6. 1).

§ 8. NOUNS AND ADJECTIVES (general)

FEMININE.	MASCULINE.	
טָבָא	טָב	singular absolute.
טָבַת	טָב	construct.
טָבְתָא	טָבָא	emphatic.
טָבָן	טָבִין	plural absolute.
טָבָת	טָבֵי	construct.
טָבָתָא	טָבַיָּא	emphatic.

Emphatic state. **1*.** The emphatic ending *ā* has a demonstrative force equivalent to the Hebrew definite article. The corresponding English expression may, however, be indefinite, e. g. when the noun is abstract (16. ii. 4, 21. 15, 24. ii. 6), or a generic word (Dan. 5. 1). Sometimes the emphatic ending has practically the force of a possessive pronoun (20. 5, where שְׂנְאֵיהּ

= 'our enemies', 24. ii. 12, where 'the stick' means 'his stick' or
'a stick').

2. In PTM and OJ the emphatic state tends to lose its distinctive definite meaning, as in Syriac, but to a much lesser extent
(14. ii. 1, 25. ii. 10, 18. ii. 2, 20. 12, 24. ii. 1, 27. 6, 25. ii. 3 and 9;
Gen. 2. 10, Exod. 1. 8, 12. 20, Josh. 2. 2, Judg. 9. 36). In PTM
emphatic forms (18. 6, 18. ii. 6, 19. ii. 3, 21. ii. 7, 27. 2) as well as
absolute forms (16. ii. 6, 17. ii. 1, 29. 1, 25. ij. 3) are associated with
the indefinite word חַד, one. In OJ the emphatic state seems to be
more often used with חַד (Gen. 1. 9, 2. 24, 27. 38, 45, 33. 13, 34. 16,
40. 5, Deut. 24. 5, Josh. 3. 12, 13, 17. 17, Judg. 6. 16, 9. 37) than the
absolute is (Gen. 1. 5, 11. 1, Deut. 28. 7, Josh. 9. 2). The MS.
evidence sometimes varies and the printed texts even have both
constructions in the same verse (Gen. 11. 6, Josh. 17. 14). In OJ
a singular indefinite object is generally expressed by the emphatic
state (Gen. 2. 8, 4. 1, 4. 17, 20. 9, 21. 8, 28. 2, 29. 2, 33. 17, Judg.
6. 26), rarely by the absolute (Judg. 6. 17). Emphatic forms are
said to be preferred in pause (Berliner, *Massorah*, p. 96, Lev. 2. 13,
Deut. 26. 7).

OTA seems always to use the emphatic form in its distinctive
sense.

3*. There are a few exceptions to the rule that a noun qualified
by a demons. adjective stands in the emphatic form (16. ii. 2). The
absolute state is employed when the associated noun is accompanied
by a numeral and a demons. adjective (28. 13). In זִמְנָא הָדָא
(Judges, *passim*) the feminine noun may be regarded as masculine in form, and so as in the emphatic state. Cf. זִמְנָא הַהִיא,
Deut. 10. 10.

4*. An attributive adjective regularly assumes an emphatic orm
when the noun it qualifies stands in the emphatic state (Gen. 1. 16,
10. 21, 27. 15, 29. 2, Deut. 3. 24, 11. 2; *Chrest.* 23. ii. 4; Dan.
3. 26, 6. 27). Cf. שְׁמֵיהּ רַבָּא (1 Sam. 12. 22), but אָרִיסִי טָב (24. ii. 13).

Absolute state.   5*. Some words and phrases employ absolute forms in a definite sense (25. ii. 3, בֵּית עָלַם 'the cemetery '). In PTM foreign words may be used definitely without the addition of an emphatic ending (16. 6 ff., 23. 4, דִּימֵס, פִּילֵי). Predicative adjectives are generally put in the absolute state (Dan. 2. 11), even when, in OJ, they translate Hebrew words with a definite article attached (Gen. 2. 11, 42. 6). A predicative adjective in the emphatic state may be considered to be a superlative (15. 8).

Construct and Genitive.   6*. In PTM construct forms, followed by genitives, have only a limited use (17. 13, עַמּוּדֵי בֵּיתָךְ). They occur most frequently as the second member of compound prepositions (לְעֵיל, בְּגוֹ, לְסוֹף, &c.) and in stereotyped phrases which are almost compound nouns, e.g. בַּר נָשׁ (28. 11), בֵּית עָלַם (25. ii. 3), מְטַמְעֵי שִׁמְשָׁא 'sunset' (22. ii. 5), פְּרוּס עַרְסִי 'my bed-cover' (29. 15).

Instead of the genitive construction PTM usually employs phrases like (a) בֵּיתָא דַּחֲבֵירֵיה, עוֹפָא דִּשְׁמַיָּא 'the birds of the sky', 'the house of his comrade', or (b) בֵּיתַהּ דְּאִמַּהּ, שְׁמֵיהּ דֶּאֱלָהָא 'the name of God', 'the house of her mother', when the expression is definite, and like (c) רִמּוֹנִין דִּדְהַב 'pomegranates of gold', when the expression is indefinite. In all these cases דְּ means 'that of' or 'those of' and governs the following noun in the genitive case (§ 7, note 3). Mixed constructions like תְּלָת מִלִּין דְּחָכְמְתָא (17. 15) and מָרֵי דְבֵיתָא (*Chrest.* 17. 7, Judg. 19. 22) occur less often.

7*. In OJ the use of a construct, followed by a genitive, is general, although the constructions of note 6 also occur. Examples: (a) Gen. 1. 14, 25, 2. 7, 12, 22. 12, Josh. 1. 8, 13, 2. 2, 4. 16, 5. 1, and frequently; (b) Gen. 30. 20; (c) Gen. 3. 21, Deut. 10. 7—נַחֲלִין דְּמַיִין.

8. In OTA the idiom of a construct followed by a genitive prevails—except in one group of cases, where the constructions of note 6 (a) and (c) are preferred. These latter constructions are generally, though not exclusively, used before or after and in combination with standing phrases, such as 'treasure-house', 'house of God', 'book of records'. Examples: בֵּית גִּנְזַיָּא דִי מַלְכָּא (Ezra 5.17), אָשַׁיָּא דִּי־בֵית אֱלָהָא (Ezra 5.16), אֶצְבְּעָן דִּי יַד־אֱנָשׁ 'fingers of a human hand' (Dan. 5.5). Cf. Ezra 4.15, 6.5, 7.12, 7.17, Dan. 2.14, 2.49, 4.26, 5.3. There are comparatively few cases of the use of these constructions as an alternative to a simple construct and genitive (Ezra 5.2, 13, 14, 7.26, Dan. 2.15, 19, 38, 41, 4.12 (= 20), 5.7 (= 16 and 29), 5.23, 24, 7.4, 6, 7 (= 19), 7.9, 10, 28). A considerable proportion of them seem to imply at least a slight emphasis (e.g. Ezra 5.14, 7.26, Dan. 2.38, 5.7 (= 16 and 29), 5.23, 7.4, 7 (= 19), 7.9, 10). 'The den of lions' is both גֹּב אַרְיָוָתָא (6.8, 13, 25) and גֻּבָּא דִּי אַרְיָוָתָא (6.17, 20).

The construction of note 6 (b) occurs in OTA about a dozen times and the words governed by דִּי are then evidently in most cases emphatic (Dan. 2.44, 3.28 f., 4.23, 6.25, 27, Ezra 5.11). Renderings such as 'the name of him who is (really) God' and 'the appearance of that fourth' are sometimes appropriate (Dan. 2.20, 3.25, 3.26).

Accusative case. 9*. In PTM the object noun has generally no distinctive mark. לְ occasionally introduces definite accusatives (15.11, 16.ii.11, 21.6, 7, 23.8, 27.6) and יָת does so rarely (15.ii.8). In OJ יָת is the regular equivalent of Hebrew אֵת and לְ seldom occurs (in Gen. 3.17 לְמֵימַר = Hebrew לְקוֹל; for Gen. 39.15 see § 36, note 11). The old accusative ending ā survives in a few adverbs of place (e.g. תְּחֹתָּא 'below'). For the accusative pronoun anticipating an object noun see § 36, note 11.

10. In OTA לְ is not infrequently associated with a definite accusative. Possibly it has a slight demonstrative or emphasizing effect.[1]

---

[1] It is prefixed to expressions for the true God (Dan. 2.19, 4.31, 34, 5.23) and the false gods (3.18, 5.4, 23; cf. 2.34), to words and phrases denoting the rulers (3.2, 6.2) and wise men of Babylon (2.12, 14, 24; 5.7), to the

Inflexional endings. 11*. The feminine singular ending יָא
is attached especially to stems that end in *ān*, hence רִיקָנְיָא (Gen.
1. 2) and פְּלָנְיָא. Feminine plural endings *āwān* and *ᵉwān* are
used by some nouns. Examples: (a) חֵילָוָן, דִּירָוָן, בֵּירָוָן, לֵילָוָן,
(b) אַתְוָן, אָתְוָן—from אָת, sign, and אַחְוָן, אֲחָוָן—from אֲחָת, sister. Cf. מָאן = מָאֵן
and סָאן = סָאֵן. See also § 10, note 21, and § 30, note 2.

12*. The plurals of אַב, אֵם, and שֹׁום are אַבְהָן, אִמְּהָן, and שְׁמָהָן,
respectively.

13*. The termination ַי is sometimes used when a noun is in the
absolute or in the emphatic state. Examples: יַמֵּי (Gen. 1. 10),
חַי (Gen. 2. 7), תּוֹרֵי (Gen. 18. 7). Such forms are specially frequent
in the case of gentilic names like כּוּתָאֵי (*Chrest.* 24. ii. 1), מִצְרָאֵי
(Exod. 12. 30), חִתָּאֵי (Josh. 1. 4), and כַּשְׂדָּאֵי (Dan. 2. 5). Dalman
compares, also, Γεθσημανῆ = שְׁמָנֵי נַּת = 'garden of oils'.

14. Words like כַּפְרָנִין (Num. 32. 4), from כְּפַר, village, and בְּנָתִין
(16. ii. 14) are examples of double plurals. For *ān* as a plural
ending see Brockelmann, *Grundriss*, vol. i, p. 450 f.

Duals. 15*. The only clear duals in PTM and OJ are תְּרֵין,
תַּרְתֵּין ('two'), and מָאתַן (200). But the ending ַיִן in words such
as עֵינִין may also be a dual ending (OTA עַיְנִין). In OTA (besides
תְּרֵין, תַּרְתֵּין, and מָאתַין) יְדַיִן, רַגְלַיִן, קַרְנַיִן, and שַׁנֵּי occur.

§ 9*. CLASSIFICATION OF NOUNS (declensions)

The following classification is made with a view to a statement
of the rules for nominal inflexion, as given in the next paragraph.
Six classes, or declensions, are distinguished.

names Shadrach, Meshach, and Abednego (2. 49, 3. 13, 22, 30; cf. 3. 27 and
3. 28) and to the name Daniel, when standing as an object by itself (2. 19,
4. 31, 34, 5. 23; cf. 2. 13 and 18). Almost the only other cases of לְ introducing
a definite object, in Daniel, are found in 5. 2, 22 and 23. In Ezra very few
examples altogether occur (4. 14, 5. 12, 6. 7, 7. 25). In Ezra 6. 7 לעבידת may
be regarded as a textual error.

A nouns. Nouns originally disyllabic and having two short vowels are very slightly distinguished in Aramaic from nouns originally monosyllabic and ending in two consonants. The two groups are here joined in the A class of nouns, which is further subdivided into three sub-classes according as the characteristic vowel (used in the inflected forms) is ă, ĭ, or ŭ (OTA ŏ). The absolute forms, of which specimens follow, do not clearly indicate the sub-class to which an A noun belongs.

ŭ *class.*	ĭ *class.*	ă *class.*	
	כְּתַף	דְּהַב	originally disyllabic.
	נְדַר	נְפַשׁ	originally monosyllabic.
קְשׁוֹט	רְחִישׁ	לְחֵים	
בֹּסֶם	עֵיגֵל	עֲבֵד	
	תְּבֵן		

In the ŭ class absolute forms like רְנוּ (Deut. 9. 20, Dan. 3. 13), בְּסַם (Exod. 30. 23), and כְּתַל (Dan. 5. 5) sometimes occur. In Dan. 5. 5 the supralinear MSS. give כֹּתֵל for the כְּתַל of MT.

Words of the ă class like לְחֵים are בְּעֵיל, חֲקֵיל, טְעֵים, מְלֵיךְ, סְעֵיר, and רְעֵים (OTA בְּעֵל, טְעַם, צְלֵם, and לְחֵם, with עֲבֵד in Dan. 2. 49, 6. 21).

Some words have more than one absolute form (חֲקַל, מֶלֶךְ, &c.). In OTA the uses of טַעַם and טְעַם, צְלָם and צְלֵם are perhaps differentiated by MT (Strack, § 8 c.).

יֵרַךְ (Num. 5. 22) and יֵחַם (Exod. 22. 21, Deut. 27. 19) are unusual forms, perhaps at first only orthographically different from יְרַךְ and יְחַם (§ 2, notes 8 and 9). The former belongs to the ĭ sub-class and the latter to the ă sub-class.

B nouns. Disyllabic nouns having ă in the final syllable and an unchangeable long vowel, or a shut syllable, in the penult, together with all participles (whose final vowel is ṣere or pathah) follow a distinct rule of inflexion (see § 10).   Examples: עָלַם, אַרְבַּע, אָמַר, סָהֵיד.   A small number of monosyllables including חַד, זַו, דַּם, יַד, בַּר (son), and שׁוֹם (OTA שֵׁם) belong to this B class and not to the C class.

C nouns. Monosyllables from stems ע״ע have absolute forms like עַם, אֵם, and כֹּל, in which the vowels ē and ō are frequently represented by ־ִ and וֹ respectively (e. g. שֵׁית, פּוֹם). Dalman gives גֵּיר (arrow) and גּוּב (pit) as variant forms in the second and third classes.

Some words which are not from ע״ע stems follow the inflexion of this class (e.g. פּוֹם, עֵז). In OTA the MSS. of MT read פֻּם (mouth), but the supralinear MSS. have פֹּם, in accordance with the analogy of גּוּב, דֹּב, &c.

D nouns. Words which remain unchanged when terminations are added to the stem are principally disyllables with a long vowel in the final syllable (e. g. עֲוִיר, גְּבַר, שְׁלָם, אֱנָשׁ), and monosyllables like טוּר, יוֹם, תּוֹר, and דִּין. The unchangeable ā in the first group is equivalent to Hebrew ō (שָׁלוֹם, &c.).

E nouns. It is convenient to make nouns from stems final yodh or final waw a separate group. Words like טְלִי are chiefly substantives and those like סָנֵי (OTA שָׁנֵא, אָתֵה) are participle forms (see § 30). Probably the orthography חֲיָו (Gen. 12. 11) is equivalent to חֲזָו (§ 2. 8).

F nouns. In this class are included all nouns with the terminations ăi (= Hebrew î) or ē added to a triliteral stem. Examples: קַדְמַי (or קַדְמָאי, § 2. 1), רְבִיעַי, תִּמְנַי. The long vowel of OTA (כַּשְׂדָּי, רְבִיעַי, קַדְמָי) is also the pausal form of OJ (Gen. 1. 13, 19).

§ 10. INFLEXION OF NOUNS (masculine types)

Emph.	Constr.	Absol.	Emph.	Constr.	Absol.	
PLURAL.			**SINGULAR.**			
מַלְכַיָּא	מַלְכֵי	מַלְכִין	מַלְכָּא	מֶלֶךְ	מֶלֶךְ	A
בַּעֲלַיָּא	בַּעֲלֵי	בַּעֲלִין	בַּעְלָא	בְּעֵיל	בְּעֵיל	
נִדְרַיָּא	נִדְרֵי	נִדְרִין	נִדְרָא	נְדַר	נְדַר	
נַהֲרַיָּא	נַהֲרֵי	נַהֲרִין	נַהֲרָא	נְהַר	נְהַר	
לִבְבַיָּא	לִבְבֵי	לִבְבִין	לִבְבָּא	לְבַב	לְבַב	
עָלְמַיָּא	עָלְמֵי	עָלְמִין	עָלְמָא	עָלַם	עָלַם	B
יְדַיָּא	יְדֵי	יְדִין	יְדָא	יַד	יַד	
עִנַּיָּא	עִנֵּי	עִנִּין	עִנָּא	עֵז	עֵז	C
גֻּבְרַיָּא	גֻּבְרֵי	גֻּבְרִין	גֻּבְרָא	גְּבַר	גְּבַר	D
טַלַיָּא	טְלֵי / טַלֵּי	¹ טְלַן / טְלִין	טַלְיָא	טְלֵי	טְלֵי	E
סַנְיַיָּא	סַנֵּי	¹ סָנַן / סָנַן	סַנְיָא	סָנֵי	סָנֵי	
חַזְוַיָּא	חַזְוֵי	חַזְוִין	חַזְוָא	חֵיזוּ	חֵיזוּ	
עִבְרַיֵּא / עִבְרָאֵי		עִבְרָיִין / עִבְרָאִין	עִבְרַיָּא / עִבְרָאָא		עִבְרַי	F
כֻּרְסָוָתָא	כֻּרְסָוָת	כֻּרְסָוָן	כֻּרְסַיָּא	כֻּרְסֵי	כֻּרְסֵי	

¹ The accent in these plurals was probably placed on the *á* and the ending may be pronounced as *ain*.

A nouns. 1*. Nouns of the A type retain or assume a monosyllabic form before inflexional endings. The usual vowels of these monosyllables are ă, ĭ, and ŭ (OTA ŏ). The mutation of the third radical of inflected forms in OTA—when the third radical is susceptible of mutation—shows that the preceding shewa is vocal (a) in the plural of nouns originally monosyllabic (מַלְכִּין), (b) in the singular and plural of nouns originally disyllabic (דְּנִבְּין, לִבְבָא). All the examples of the table above are treated according to this rule, although the Yemenite MSS. with supralinear punctuation do not indicate vocal shewa, except after a medial guttural, and even then not consistently (e.g. נַהְרָא, Gen. 2. 13, but נַהֲרָא, Josh. 1. 4).

2. Under the influence of medial *p, b,* and *m* (labials) ŭ is often substituted for ă and ĭ in the monosyllabic stems of the first and second sub-classes, especially in PTM. Examples: רֻמְשָׁא, גֻּבְרָא, גֻּפְנָא, דֻּבְשָׁא. The absolute form גֻּפֵן, for גֻּפֵן, may be regarded as a secondary formation from the inflected stem *gufn.* In OTA the plural forms of גְּבַר are always גֻּבְרִין, &c.

3. The vowel ĭ is also frequently substituted for an original ă. Examples: דְּבְחָא, שְׁמַשָּׁא, מְטַרָא, דְּכְרָא, בְּסְרָא; OTA זִמְנָא, בִּשְׂרָא, נִשְׁרִין, דְּבְחִין, שְׁמַשָּׁא. The absolute form דֵּיבַח (Exod. 12. 27) may be a secondary formation like גֻּפֵן. The stem vowel of the inflected forms of רֶגֶל is ĭ in the supralinear MSS. of OTA and according to the Babylonian tradition (Kahle; cf. *Chrest.* 15. 9). The MT of Daniel and the Yemenite MSS. of OJ give ă (Josh. 5. 15, 14. 9).

4. In the ĭ sub-class, nouns whose initial radical is a guttural generally retain ḥireq in the inflected forms. חֶלְמָא from חֵלֶם (dream), in the MT of Daniel and in some OJ MSS., may be due to Hebrew influence (cf. עֶגְלִי, &c.). Ḥireq and seghol also interchange in the OTA group נֶּשְׁמְהוֹן, נִּשְׁמַהּ, נִּשְׁמֵהּ.

5. In the ŭ sub-class, when ḥolem occurs as the vowel of the inflected stem it may be understood to represent ŏ (§ 2. 1). Examples: אוֹרְחָא Gen. 38. 16, קוּבְעִין Exod. 28. 40, עוֹרְבָא Lev.

11. 15 (Dalman, p. 144). According to the punctuation of MT there are three examples of ŏ-stems in OTA (Dan. 2. 37, 4. 12, 6. 20) and one of an ŭ-stem (כְּתָלַיָּא) Ezra 5. 8). Similarly the feminine חֲכְמָא is written חָכְמָא in MT and in some late MSS. of OJ. In Dan. 4. 34 and 5. 23 the supralinear punctuation is אָרְחָה, and the MSS. of MT are divided between that and אָרְחָה or אֲרְחָה. In OJ inflected forms like מְעוּגֵי (Josh. 2. 6) for מְעָגֵי sometimes occur.

6*. In the supralinear MSS. of OJ nouns like בַּיִת and עַיִן, in the construct singular and in the inflected stems, nearly always have forms like בֵּית (Dalman, p. 91, note 1). In MT construct singulars are like עֵין and inflected stems like עֵינִין, although the supralinear MSS. often substitute ē for ai, especially when pronominal suffixes are joined to the stem (see Strack's note on Dan. 4. 1). בָּתִּין is the plural of בַּיִת. חֵיל is used as an absolute form (Exod. 32. 12).

B nouns. **7*.** The final stem vowel of nouns of the B class becomes vocal shewa when terminations are added to the stem. For some apparent exceptions see § 21, note 6.

C nouns. **8*.** In nouns of the C class the final radical is doubled before inflexional endings and the stem vowel is normally ă or ĭ or ŭ, according to the vowel of the uninflected stem (עַמָּא, גֻּבָּא, אֻמָּא). Before final resh the stem vowel is lengthened in compensation, when doubling does not take place (hence בָּרָא from בַּר (country)). Some nouns put ĭ for ă in the inflected forms (פֻּם, פֻּמָּא). In OTA אֶשָּׁא, from אֵשׁ, is unique (Dan. 7. 11); in OJ אֶשָּׁא (fem. absolute) is also used.

9*. In OJ, although the stem vowel of the word כֹּל with pronominal suffixes (§ 12, note 6) is always ŭ, the emphatic form is regularly כּוֹלָּא (Josh. 11. 19), pointed in Berliner's *Onkelos* sometimes with daghesh (Exod. 29. 24, Lev. 8. 27) and sometimes without (Gen. 6. 19, 20, 16. 12, Lev. 1. 9). In Lev. 8. 27 Berliner prints כּוּלָּא. In OTA the MSS. of MT always have כֹּלָּא (five

times), and the supralinear MSS. agree (Dan. 4. 25). Ḥolem in
this and similar words denotes a short vowel (§ 2. 1). The reading
חוֹמָא (= חֹמָא) in Gen. 8. 22 (Dalman, p. 145) is an alternative to
חֵמָא (cf. Berliner).

10*. In the later Yemenite MSS. of OJ Hebrew כָּל־ is represented by כֹּל and Hebrew כֹּל by כֹּל. In Gen. 1–2 (Merx), Josh. 1–2,
and Judg. 1–2 (Praetorius) the only exceptions to this rule are in
Gen. 1. 30 and Judg. 2. 15. In OTA, MT has both כָּל־ and כֹּל,
generally the former. Strack's supralinear MSS. (except G, once)
either insert no vowel or read כֹּל.

11. Plurals of the form עַמְמִין occur in OJ, PTM, and OTA
(cf. § 35, note 4).

12. Erroneous dissimilation of the doubled consonant of the
stem takes place in חַנְגִין (Exod. 32. 19), from חַג (cf. § 26, note 9).
The form אַנְפִּין (Dan. 2. 46) is also a dissimilated form.

D nouns. 13*. In this class the absolute form and the inflected
stem are identical. The inflected forms of the word שְׁלִים (Gen.
6. 9) seem, however, to be taken from a stem of the A class
(שַׁלְמִין, &c.).

E nouns. 14*. When a termination is added to words of the
E class the stem of words like טְלִי is either like טְלַי or an A stem,
with yodh as the third radical, and the inflected stem of words like
סָנִי is either like סָנַי or a B stem (see particulars in table above).
In forms like סָנְיָא and מִשְׁתְּיָא, from מִשְׁתֵּי, the shewa following
the middle radical is vocal (§ 30, note 3). In טַלְיָא it may be
treated as silent, on the analogy of the originally monosyllabic
A stems.

15*. טְלִין is contracted from טְלַיִן and סָבַן from סָבַיִן. Adjectives of
the form טְלִי have contracted plurals of the form טְלִן (Deut. 6. 11).
The only case of such an adjective in OTA has an uncontracted
plural (שָׂרַיִן, Dan. 3. 25).

16. פֵּירִין (Hebrew פְּרִי) is used in the plural only. For plurals in *āwān* see note 21. Dalman (p. 192) regards the supralinear punctuation of absolute plurals like נַּדְיִין as incorrect.

17*. When E nouns employ an A stem (as in טַלְיָא) the vowel of the stem is usually *ă*, but sometimes *ĭ* or *ŭ* (OTA *ŏ*). Examples: רִחְיָא from רְחִי, פּוּתְיָא from פְּתִי. The supralinear pathaḥ of חַזְוָא in OJ may be interpreted as seghol, in agreement with OTA חֶזְוָא (§ 2. 6).

18. Forms like חֲזוּ, חֶזְוָא, with consonantal waw, are unusual. Most nouns ending in וּ are feminine (בְּעוּ, רְבוּ) and are inflected according to the rules of § 11.

F nouns. **19*.** In the inflected forms of *ai* stems the yodh of the termination is consonantal and the preceding vowel (in OJ) is lengthened. Instead of yodh, aleph is often written (cp. § 23, note 9). The emphatic plural termination is contracted from aiya to *ē* (יָ־ or אָ־). The inflected forms of stems terminating in *ē* (תְּמֵי, בּוּרְסֵי) are treated like those of סָנֵי (E class).

EF nouns. **20.** A few words from stems with final yodh are treated like nouns of the F class in OJ (Dalman, p. 156 ε) and OTA (עֲנָן, Dan. 4. 24, from עֲנֵי). See also § 12, note 8.

21*. Some words of the E and F classes have plurals in *āwān* or *ᵉwān*, with or without retention of consonantal yodh. Examples: אָסְוָן, רָעֲוָן, בּוּרְסָן, אַרְיָוָן (cf. § 8, note 11 and § 30, note 2).

OTA. **22.** The general rules for the inflexion of nouns given in this section apply to OTA. As the E class is very slightly represented there it may be passed over by those who begin their Aramaic reading in OTA. For these the most important notes in this section are 1, 7, 8, 13, and 19, along with 3, 6, and 9 for some details.

§ 11.* INFLEXION OF NOUNS (with feminine endings)

PLURAL			SINGULAR			
Emphat.	*Const.*	*Absol.*	*Emphat.*	*Const.*	*Absol.*	
מַלְכְּתָא	מַלְכָת	מַלְכָן	מַלְכְּתָא	מַלְכַּת	מַלְכָּא	A
בְּנִשְׁתָא	בְּנִשַׁת	בְּנִשָׁן	בְּנִשְׁתָּא	בְּנִשַׁת	בְּנִשָׁא	
אִמְּרָתָא	אִמְּרָת	אִמְּרָן	אִמְּרְתָא	אִמְּרַת	אִמְּרָא	B
מִלַּיָא	מִלֵּי	מִלִּין	מִלְּתָא	מִלַּת	מִלָּא	C
מְנִירָתָא	מְנִירָת	מְנִירָן	מְנִירְתָא	מְנִירַת	מְנִירָא	D
חֵיוָתָא	חֵיוָת	חֵיוָן	חֵיוְתָא	חֵיוַת	חֵיוָא	
טַלְיָתָא	טַלְיָת	טַלְיָן	טַלְיָתָא oj	טַלִּיַת	טַלְיָא	E
			טַלִּיתָא PTM			
סָנְיָתָא	סָנְיָת	סָנְיָן	סָנְיָתָא	סָנְיַת	סָנְיָא	
גָּלְוָתָא	גָּלְוָת	גָּלְוָן	גָּלוּתָא	גָּלוּת	גָּלוֹ	
צַלְוָתָא	צַלְוָת	צַלְוָן	צְלוֹתָא	צְלוֹת	צְלוֹ	
מְנָוָתָא	מְנָוָת	מְנָוָן	מְנָתָא	מְנָת	מְנָת	
עֶבְרְיָתָא	—	עֶבְרְיָן	עֶבְרִיתָא	—	עֶבְרְיָא	F
			עֶבְרֵייתָא	—	עֶבְרְאָא	
זַרְעֲיָתָא	זַרְעֲיָת	זַרְעֲיָן	זַרְעִיתָא	זַרְעִית	זַרְעִי	G
מַלְכְּוָתָא	מַלְכְוָת	מַלְכְוָן	מַלְכֻוּתָא	מַלְכֻות	מַלְכֻו	

Aramaic of OJ and PTM

1. The stem syllables of nouns to which the feminine ending *ā*
is attached are treated in accordance with the rules of § 10. There
are, therefore, six classes of feminine nouns corresponding to the
classes of § 9. In the E class nouns having final consonantal waw
are numerous and several types of absolute singular are in use (see

Table). Abstract feminine nouns having an ending in *ī* or *ū* are treated as a separate class (G). The rules of § 10 sufficiently explain the forms of classes A–D and F, except those of the emphatic singular, which, therefore, receive special notice in what follows.

A nouns. 2. The emphatic singular ending of the A class is usually תָּ֫א, joined to the monosyllabic stem. Examples: מַלְכְּתָא, נִשְׁמָתָא, בִּרְכְּתָא. תָּא is added to the stem קְטַל in the case of some nouns having stems originally disyllabic (parallel to Hebrew words like צְדָקָה). Examples (from Dalman): צְוָחְתָּא, אֲדַמְתָּא, נְדַבְתָּא, צִדְקְתָא, חֲבַרְתָּא בְּנִשְׁתָּא (absolute בְּנִשָׁא). Berliner's *Onkelos* gives עֶגְלְתָא (Deut. 21. 4, 6) for 'calf' (from עֶגְלָא), as well as for 'wagon' (Num. 7. 3, from עֲגָלָא). The emphatic sing. fem. of חֲדַת (= חֲדָשׁ) is חֲדַתָּא.

The absolute singular feminine of a stem originally disyllabic is distinguished in OTA from a stem originally monosyllabic by the vocal shewa following the middle radical (כִּדְבָה, Dan. 2. 9), and this analogy may be followed in reading OJ and PTM (cf. § 10, note 1). In all feminine plurals of the A class the shewa following the middle radical may be treated as vocal (§ 10, note 1).

B nouns. 3. In this class the emphatic ending is תָּא and is joined to the absolute stem of § 9 (אִמַּרְתָּא, יְלִידְתָּא, יְתִיבְתָּא—see under D nouns, below). But the emphatic form of בְּרָא 'daughter', is בְּרַתָּא, and that of שְׁנָא 'year', is שַׁתָּא.

C nouns. 4. In the C class תָּ֫א is joined to the stem used by all the inflected forms. מִלָּא, like many feminine nouns, has plurals of the masculine form. שֵׁינָא 'sleep', although not from an ע״ע stem, is inflected like words of this group (שְׁנָתָא, &c.)

D nouns. 5. With unchangeable stems the emphatic ending, according to the supralinear punctuation, is usually תָּ֫א (דְּרָתָא, תַּקִּיפְתָּא, שְׁבוּעֲתָא, עֲבִידְתָּא, בִּיעֲתָא, שָׁעֲתָא). תָּא is used only with a few disyllabic stems whose final vowel is *ē* or *ū* (שְׁפֵילְתָּא, גְּנוּבְתָּא, מְהוּלְתָּא). יְלִידְתָּא and יְתִיבְתָּא belong rather to the B class.

Certain nouns, which might be expected to belong to the A class, have forms of the D type (נְבִילָא ; כְּנִישְׁתָא , כְּנִישָׁא ; שְׁאֵילְתָא , שְׁאֵילָא ; נְבֵילְתָא , דְּבֵילָא ,(דִּבֵילְתָא), although not exclusively (cf. נְבְלַת, Lev. 5. 2, and לִבְנִין, Exod. 5. 7). All have close parallels in Hebrew.

E nouns. 6. There is considerable variety in the inflected forms of feminine nouns of this declension. In the טַלְיָא group yodh is always consonantal in OJ and the stem resembles that of the A declension. In PTM quiescence of the yodh takes place in the emphatic sing. (see Table). In the סָנֵי group, both in OJ and PTM, yodh quiesces in the construct and emphatic of the singular.

A few nouns have consonantal waw in the singular. Examples: רַעֲוָא (Gen. 4. 5) and קִרְיָא or קִרְוָא 'city' (emphatic קַרְתָּא, plural קִרְוִין). A larger number have consonantal waw in the plural only. For the various forms of the absolute singular and for their inflexions see table of nouns above. Other examples of the group are טֵיבוּ, קְצָת, רְשׁוּ, רְבוּ, זָכוּ. The rare absolute sing. of the word used in OJ for Hebrew עוֹלָה seems to be עֲלָא (Isai. 40. 16). The construct is עֲלַת (Lev. 9. 17, Merx), the emphatic עֲלָתָא (Josh. 22. 23, Judg. 6. 26) and the plural עֲלָוָן (Mic. 6. 6, Merx). Berliner's עָלָת &c. are erroneous. Cf. Syriac and OTA (note 11).

In all feminine plurals of the E class the shewa following the middle radical may be treated as vocal, according to the analogy of §10, note 1.

F nouns. 7. After the diphthong *āi* the emphatic termination is תָא, with mutated ת, but without vocal shewa preceding. Usually the vowel before תָא is *ê*. Supralinear plurals like עֲבְרַיָתָא Dalman (p. 79) treats as erroneous.

עֲוָיָא (= Hebrew עָוֹן) generally, and perhaps always, used in the plural (עֲוָיָן, &c.), is a feminine noun similar to the OTA masculine forms עֲנֵי and פְּתֵי (§ 10, note 20).

G nouns. 8. The vowel terminations of the singular are replaced by consonantal yodh or waw in the plural (see Table). The mutation of the third radical in the plural is a peculiar feature.

Old Testament Aramaic

A, B, and C nouns.   **9.** The inflexion of feminine nouns in OTA is the same as in OJ, except in the emphatic singular of nouns of the D class.

There is only one OTA example of the ending תָא in the A class, viz. יַבֶּשְׁתָּא (Dan. 2. 10). It appears in the supralinear punctuation of OJ as יַבֶּשְׁתָּא (Gen. 1. 9) or יְבֶּשְׁתָּא (§ 2. 6). Emphatic singulars of the B and C classes are אִגַּרְתָּא (Ezra 4. 11), רַבְּתָא (Dan. 4. 27), and מִלְּתָא (Dan. 2. 8).

D nouns.   **10.** In MT all words having unchangeable disyllabic stems receive תָא as their emphatic singular ending (עֲבִידְתָּא, שְׁאֵלְתָּא, גְּבוּרְתָּא, יְקָרְתָּא [1] מָרָדְתָּא, &c.). The two words having unchangeable monosyllabic stems, חֵיוְתָא (Dan. 4. 11) and בִּירְתָא (Ezra 6. 2), both receive the emphatic ending תָא. (for the reading בִּירְתָא see Ginsburg and Strack). MT שָׁעֲתָא (Dan. 3. 6, &c.), although supported by some supralinear MSS., should be corrected into שָׁעֲתָא and included in the D class.

E nouns.   **11.** There are very few inflected forms of the E class in OTA. קִרְיְתָא (Ezra 4. 12) and עֲרְוַת (Ezra 4. 14) belong to the טַלְיָא group, שְׁנָין (Dan. 7. 3) to the (פְּלָה) סָגִי group, and עֲלָוָן (Ezra 6. 9) to the מְנָת group. כִּנְוָת, from כְּנָת, occurs several times with pronominal suffixes. גָּלוּתָא (Dan. 2. 25), from גְּלוֹ, is also a noun of this declension.

F nouns.   **12.** Before the emphatic singular ending, instead of *āï*, as in קַדְמָיְתָא (Dan. 7. 4), רְבִיעָיְתָא (Dan. 7. 19), some MSS. read *ăï* (cf. note 7). Shewa after *āï* is silent (note 7) in spite of metheg (קַדְמָיְתָא). עֲנָיָא (see note 7) occurs once in the plural with a pronominal suffix (Dan. 4. 24).

G nouns.   **13.** מַשְׁרוֹקִיתָא (Dan. 3. 5) is an inflected form of the *ī* group and מַלְכְוָתָא (Dan. 2. 44) an example of the *ū* group.

---

[1] If reckoned a participle, this word comes under the rule of the B class.

§ 12. PRONOMINAL SUFFIXES (with singular nouns)

1*. For the usual forms of the suffixes in OJ and PTM see § 4 and for those of OTA see paradigm, p. 93.

2*. אָב, אָח, and חָם with pronominal suffixes are treated as follows:

אֲחוּהָא	אֲחוּהִי	אֲחוּיִךְ / אֲחוּךְ	אֲחוּךְ	אָחִי
אֲחוּהֵין	אֲחוּהוֹן	אֲחוּכֵין	אֲחוּכוֹן	אֲחוּנָא OJ / אֲחוּנַן PTM

The suffixes הִי, הָא, נַן, נָא, and יךְ are all unaccented. Regarding the first three see further § 13, note 2. יִךְ is said to have been preferred by the school of Sura and ךְ (2 s. f.) by the school of Nehardea (Berliner, *Massorah*, p. 62 f.) The former is given by Merx (Gen. 24. 23) and in Berliner's *Onkelos* (Gen. 20. 16, 38. 11), the latter in Praetorius (Judg. 14. 15, Josh. 2. 18) and Lagarde (2 Sam. 6. 21, 13. 17).

3. For אֲבִי OJ uses אַבָּא (Gen. 44. 32, Judg. 14. 16, 1 Kings 2. 32, cf. Rom. 8. 15, ἀββᾶ). אִמָּא ' my mother ' is a similar form (Judg. 14. 16). Dalman explains the ending as originally *ă*, from an older *ai*, and so as really the pronominal suffix for ' my '. In Dan. 5. 13 אַבִּי (MT) may originally have meant אֲבִי (§ 2. 7), which is the reading of the supralinear MSS. אֲבוּהִי is sometimes contracted into אֲבוּי (*Chrest.* 18. 12).

A nouns. 4*. The stems of masculine nouns with pronominal suffixes attached are generally formed according to the rules of § 10, with some slight modifications.

In the A class the distinction between מַלְכָּא and לְבְבָּא is paralleled by the distinction between מַלְכִּי and לְבְבִּי. Before heavy suffixes, words ending in a guttural or resh commonly use a stem of the קְטַל type. E. g. אַרְעֲהוֹן (Josh. 10. 42), בְּסַרְכוֹן (Judg. 8. 7), but also בְּסִרְכוֹן (Judg. 9. 2).

The statement of § 10, note 6, applies also to stems with suffixes attached (hence OJ בֵּיתֵיהּ, OTA בַּיְתֵהּ). In Dan. 4. 1 the MSS. are divided between בֵּיתִי and בַּיְתִי. For לַיְת with suffixes see § 15, notes 2 and 3.

B nouns. 5*. In the B class the stem vowel of the final syllable is retained before heavy suffixes and becomes vocal shewa before light suffixes. Examples: יַדְהוֹן, יָדִי, מֵימְרֵהוֹן, מֵימְרִי (OTA יְדְהֹם).

C nouns. 6*. The supralinear orthography represented by כֻּלֵּיהּ is normal, although the vowel *u* is short (§ 2. 1). In OTA כֹּל with suffixes has *ŏ* as its stem vowel (Dan. 2. 38, 7. 19), while all other words of this class have *ŭ*.

E nouns. 7*. In the E class words like טְלֵי use their emphatic stem before all suffixes. In the *ŭ* sub-class the later Yemenite MSS. sometimes make the vowel of the inflected stem *ŏ*, as in MT (Dan. 4. 9). Examples: חָלְיִי, טַלְיְהוֹן, טַלְיִי (Judg. 9. 11), עָפְיֵהּ (Dan. 4. 9). Participle forms like סָנֵי and nouns like מִשְׁתֵּי and מְשָׁרֵי either employ their emphatic stem (מִשְׁתֵּיהּ, בְּרִיךְ) or, more generally, are treated as plural nouns are (§ 13, note 7). For participles see further § 30, note 4.

F nouns. 8. Words from stems final yodh that belong to the F class (§ 10, note 20) like דְּוִי (OJ) and פְּתִי (OTA), have suffixed forms like דְּוָיִי (Gen. 35. 18, Dalman) and פְּתָיֵהּ (Dan. 3. 1). Nouns like כּוּרְסֵי with suffixes are treated as plural nouns (§ 13, note 7).

Feminine stems. 9*. Feminine nouns to which pronominal suffixes are attached may be arranged in three divisions, according as the termination of the emphatic singular is תָּא, תָּ. or תָא.

(1) Nouns that use the ending תָּא join suffixes to the emphatic stem (צִדְקָתְכוֹן, אִמַּרְתִּי).

(2) In the case of nouns whose emphatic ending is תָּ., light suffixes are united to the emphatic stem and heavy suffixes to the construct stem (מִלָּתְהוֹן; מַלְכַּתְהוֹן, מַלְכָּתִי, מִלְּתִי; עֲבִידַתְהוֹן, טַלְיְתִי; טַלְיָתְהוֹן, עֲבִידְתִי).

(3) Nouns of the E, F, and G classes, whose emphatic ending is
תָא, add suffixes to the emphatic or construct stems, which
are the same (מַלְכּוּתִי, מְנָתְהוֹן, גָּלוּתֵיהּ). For examples
of F nouns see § 29, note 9.

10. שֶׁנְתֵּהּ (Dan. 6. 19) may be regarded as a noun of the C class,
rather than as derived from an absolute form שְׁנָא (cf. § 11, note 4).

Feminine suffixes. **11.** The supralinear MSS. of OJ generally
write the suffixes of the 2 plur. masc. and of the 3 plur. masc.
instead of the corresponding feminine forms (Dalman). The same
substitution is often made in PTM.

§ 13. PRONOMINAL SUFFIXES (with masc. plur. stems).

PLURAL SUFFIXES.		SINGULAR SUFFIXES.		
PTM	OJ	PTM	OJ	
ـֵינַן	ـָנָא	ـַי, אַי	ـַי	1 com.
ـֵיכוֹן	ـֵיכוֹן	ـָיִךְ, ـָךְ	ـָךְ	2 masc.
ـֵיכֵין	ـֵיכֵין	יכִי, יִךְ	ـְכִי, ـֵיךְ	fem.
			ـְכִי, ـֵךְ	
ـֵיהוֹן	ـֵיהוֹן	וֹהִי, וֹי	וֹהִי	3 masc.
ـֵיהֵין	ـֵיהֵין	ـֶיהָא, ـֶיה, ـָה	ـָהָא	fem.

Suffix forms. **1*.** אַי, יִךְ, and יכִי are simply orthographical
variants for ـַי, יִךְ, and ـְכִי. For ـְכִי and ـֶיהָא see § 2. 14. ـָא is
an alternative in OJ for ـַי (see § 29, note 8).

2*. The 'connective vowel' of these pronominal suffixes was
originally the plural ending *ai*, which in a majority of cases has
become *ē* or *ă* or *ā*. The connective *ō* of וֹהִי is explained either as
a nominative plural ending = *au* (Barth) or as a dissimilation from
ai (Dalman). The terminations כִי, הִי, and הָא were originally used
with singular as well as with plural stems (§ 4, note 2, § 12, note 2).
The contracted forms of 3 sing. masc. and 3 sing. fem. are charac-

teristic of PTM. נַן is a reduplicated ending found also in Syriac. The suffix ן_ is used by PTM in רַבָּנַן 'our teachers'.

3. In OTA the Kᵉthibh implies the earlier pronunciations יְךּ, יהֵ_, and יְנָא_, which the Qᵉre alters into ךְ_, הֵ_, and נָא_ respectively. See paradigm, p. 93.

4*. It may be observed that several of the *ai* suffixes attached to plural stems are identical with the suffix forms attached to singular nouns (ךְ_, הֵ_, נָא_). Unvocalized יה in PTM, when joined to a masc. plural stem means 'her', and to a singular stem 'his'.

Plural stems. **5*.** Most of the plural stems of § 10 are also used when pronominal suffixes are joined to plurals (e. g. מַלְכַּיָּא, גֻּבְּרַי, יְדַי). Only the טְלֵי group of E nouns employs with suffixes as its plural stem a stem identical with that of the emphatic singular (טַלְיֵיהוֹן, טַלְיַי). In other E nouns *ai* suffixes are joined directly to the ordinary plural stem (מִשְׁרֵיהוֹן, רָעֵיהוֹן, סָנַי). In Dan. 2. 32 this treatment is extended to the form חָדוֹהִי, although presumably its uninflected singular is חֲדַי, as in OJ.

6. For 'they two' OJ always uses תַּרְוֵיהוֹן (Gen. 2. 25), instead of תְּרֵיהוֹן, and PTM sometimes has the same form (cf. § 8, note 15).

Singular stems like plurals. **7*.** The direct combination of pronominal suffixes with the singular ending *ē* of certain nouns of the E class, like מִשְׁתֵּי and מִשְׁרֵי, produces a set of *ai* suffixes, which are precisely the same as those attached to plural stems. This makes the singular and plural forms of such nouns frequently indistinguishable (מָחוֹהִי, מִשְׁרֵיהוֹן). For the case of participles see § 30, note 4, and for infinitives § 29, note 8. Certain F nouns, like כֻּרְסֵי, are also combined with suffixes in the manner of plural stems.

8. מָרֵי 'master', with suffixes employs a stem with consonantal yodh (מָרְיָךְ, *Chrest.*, p. 23, note 1), or a contracted stem with the suffixes of § 12 (מָרֵיהּ, Exod. 21. 29, מָרִי, Dan. 4. 16, 21) or a contracted stem with the suffixes of this section (מָרוֹהִי, Exod. 21. 34).

In the Kᵉthibh form מראי (Dan. 4.16, 21) אַי might represent *ai*
(§ 2.1) but probably א stands for consonantal yodh (§ 23, n. 9).

9*. Prepositions that originally ended in *ē*, for that reason take
ai suffixes (עֲלִי, עֲלָךְ, &c.), and other prepositions do so by analogy
(קֳדָמַי, בָּתְרַי). In OTA עֲלַיְנָא or עֲלֶינָא (Ezra 4. 12, &c.), an old
form of the suffix נָא_, is preserved (cf. note 3).

Fem. plur. suffixes. 10. The observations of § 12, note 11,
apply also to the suffixes added to plural stems.

§ 14*. PRONOMINAL SUFFIXES (with fem. plur. stems).

BORROWED *ai* SUFFIXES.		NORMAL SUFFIXES.		
PTM	OJ	OJ and PTM		
	אִמְּרָתַי	אִמְּרָתְנָא OJ	אִמְּרָתִי	1 com.
		אִמְּרָתַן PTM		
אִמְּרָתֵיכוֹן	—	אִמְּרָתְכוֹן	אִמְּרָתָךְ	2 masc.
	אִמְּרָתָךְ	—	אִמְּרָתִיךְ	fem.
אִמְּרָתֵיהוֹן	אִמְּרָתוֹהִי	אִמְּרָתְהוֹן	אִמְּרָתֵיה	3 masc.
	אִמְּרָתְהָא	—	אִמְּרָתַה	fem.

The normal suffixes added to feminine plural stems are identical
with those added to singular stems and the noun form employed
is the construct or the emphatic stem, which are the same. The
Hebrew practice of combining with feminine plural stems the
suffixes appropriate to masc. plural stems, and derived from them
(צִדְקוֹתַי, &c.) is occasionally followed in OJ and PTM (for particulars see Table above). Dalman gives the order of frequency of
occurrence of these borrowed *ai* suffixes in OJ as: (1) 3 sing. fem.,
(2) 1 sing., (3) 3 sing. masc. הָ_ for יָ_ occurs only once or twice, in
the Targum of Jonathan (Dalman, p. 205 f.). In Dan. 2. 23 some
MSS. read אֲבָהָתִי for אֲבָהָתִי (§ 8, note 12), and this is the only
exception to the general rule in OTA.

§ 15. לֵית, אִית, ETC.

Forms. 1. Both in OJ (Lev. 11. 26) and PTM (25. ii. 12) לָא
אִית occurs for לֵית. In OTA the forms used are אִיתַי and לָא אִיתַי.

Subject pronouns. 2. In PTM the subject pronouns of
these particles are in the nominative forms (e.g. לֵית הוּא). לֵית
coalesces with the pronouns of the 1 sing. and 1 plur. and 3 plur.
into the compounds לֵינָא, לֵינַן, and לֵיתְנוּן.

3. In OJ the subject pronouns are generally expressed by
suffixes, except in the 3 person plural. The suffixes are *ai* suffixes,
because of the original ending of the particles (cf. § 13, note 7, and
OTA אִיתַי). In the 1 person singular the ending *ai* has become *ă*
and the suffix adopts an accusative form (§ 36, note 1). Examples:
אִיתֵיכוֹן, אִיתוֹהִי, אִיתַנִי. The inflected stem of לֵית has two forms, as
in לְיתוֹהִי and לְיָתוֹהִי. In the latter the shewa following yodh is
vocal (Dalman, p. 108). The nominative form of the pronoun of
the 3 person plural coalesces with לֵית, as in PTM (לֵיתְנוּן). The
nominatives of other persons are also sometimes used in OJ (Deut.
1. 9 לֵית אֲנָא יָכָל).

4. In OTA the subject pronouns of אִיתַי are expressed by means
of suffixes of the *ai* form (אִיתֵיכוֹן, &c.).

Usages. 5. אִית and לֵית express 'there is' and 'there are'
(there is not, there are not); e.g. אִית הָכָא חַד יְהוּדָי 'there is here a
Jew' (20. 9). They are regularly combined with לִי, לָךְ, &c., to
express the verb 'have'; e.g. אִין לֵית לָךְ פְּרִיטִין 'if you have no
money' (15. 9). Sometimes אִית may be rendered by 'it is',
e.g. לָא אִית בְּחֵילִי 'it is not in my power' (25. ii. 12). In OJ לֵית is
used absolutely, like Hebrew אֵין (Gen. 5. 24, 37. 30).

6. With a predicate, which may be a noun, adjective, or participle, these particles are equivalent to the English copula; e.g. לֵית
אֲנָא מֶלֶךְ 'I am not a king' (20. 10), לֵית בֵּיתָא הָדֵין חָרֵב 'this house
will not be destroyed' (20. 12). A subject noun or pronoun follows
אִית (לֵית), except in relative sentences or for the sake of emphasis.

Before prepositional phrases, where אִית may also be translated
'is', it really has the sense of 'there is' or 'there exists', e.g. כָּל
מָה דְּאִית בַּהּ 'everything that is (there is) in it' (26. 14; cf. Dan.
2. 30).

§ 16. VERBAL STEMS

REFLEXIVE AND PASSIVE.		ACTIVE.		
אִתְכְּתִיב	Ithpeel	כְּתַב	Peal	Simple
אִתְכַּתַּב	Ithpaal	כַּתִּיב	Pael	Intensive
אִתַּכְתַּב	Ittaphal	אַכְתִּיב	Aphel	Causative

1*. The stems having preformative *ith* are reflexives, which serve
also as passives.

2*. The Pael, Aphel, and Ithpeel of verbs final ה, ח, and ע take
pathaḥ for ṣere in the final syllable. For other variations caused
by the influence of gutturals see § 23.

Peal.   **3*.** Peal perfects with *ē* or *ū* in the final syllable, principally intransitive, occur especially in OJ. Examples: תְּקִיף 'be
strong' (Gen. 1. 28) or 'be angry' (Gen. 4. 5), דְּחֵיל (Gen. 3. 10),
קְרִיב (Gen. 12. 1), שְׁאֵיל (Judg. 1. 1), שְׁלֵים (Gen. 15. 16), נְסַב and
נְסִיב (Gen. 2. 21); דְּמַךְ and דְּמוּךְ (Gen. 2. 21). *ō* occurs for *ū*
(מְרוֹד, Kahle, p. 219) and *ī* for *ē*, especially in pause (Dalman,
pp. 54 f., 257). In OTA *ē* and *ī* both occur, the latter generally in
pause (תְּקִף, שְׁאֵל, קְרֵב). Where MT has *ī* the supralinear MSS.
sometimes have *ē* (Dan. 6. 21, וְעַל).

Haphel.   **4*.** Haphels sometimes take the place of Aphels
in PTM and OJ. The only examples in OJ are הֵימִן, הוֹדַע, and
הוֹפַע (Dalman). For OTA Haphels see note 11.

5. In הימין, which is borrowed from Hebrew, the final vowel is *ī*
(Gen. 45. 26—Berliner) or *ē* (Gen. 15. 6—Berliner). Supralinear
MSS. give both הֵימִן (Dalman, p. 302, note 2) and הֵימֵן (Merx).
In Dan. 6. 24 the sublinear vowel is *ī* and the supralinear is *ē*.

Ith forms. **6*.** The Ithpᵉel and Ithpaal of verbs initial dental and sibilant are modified as follows

(*a*) ת of the prefix is assimilated to a following ת, ט, or ד (thus אִתְדַּבַּר becomes אִדַּבַּר).

(*b*) ת changes places with a following sibilant and after צ and ז becomes ט and ד respectively. Examples : אִצְטְרַךְ, אִשְׁתַּמַּע, אִזְדְּרַע.

Ittaphal forms are not affected (אִתַּסְהַד, Exod. 21. 29).

7. In PTM assimilation of ת to פ, ב, מ, נ and other consonants takes place occasionally. Examples : אִתְבְּרִי = אִבְּרִי, אִתְפְּסִיק = אִפְּסִיק, אִתְנְשַׁמַת = אִנְּשַׁמַת (28. 4), אִתְמְלִיךְ = אִמְּלִיךְ (21. 4). Dalman compares ἐφφαθά (Mark 7. 34) = אֶתְפְּתַח (§ 19, note 5). Cf. also *Chrest.* 4. 19, מִתְקַנְיָה = מִקַּנְיָה.

8. In the supralinear vocalization an intrusive vowel frequently appears after preformative את, in the perfect and other tenses (אִתִימְנַע).

Shaphel, &c. **9*.** Shaphel causative forms are found. The most frequent are שַׁכְלִיל 'complete' (passive אִשְׁתַּכְלַל, Gen. 2. 1), שַׁעֲבֵיד 'subdue' (Gen. 12. 5), שֵׁיזִיב 'rescue' (Gen. 37. 21), שֵׁיצִי 'finish' (Gen. 2. 2). See § 26, note 6.

10. Less common forms are the Pōʻēl and Pāʻēl (both = Arabic iii), with their passives (e. g. זַמִּין, Gen. 24. 14). The Pōlēl, Pālēl, and Palpēl are formed from stems ע״וּ and ע״ע (§ 32, note 7, § 34, note 2).

OTA. **11.** OTA instead of Ittaphals uses Hophals and a perfect passive Pᵉal of the form Pᵉʻīl, especially in the 3 person (יְהִיבַת. Dan. 5. 28 ; יְהִיבוּ, Ezra 5. 14 ; cf. אֲחִידַת, *Chrest.* 1. 8). Haphels for Aphels and preformative הַת for אַת are both normal in OTA, though not universal. With אֶשְׁתּוֹמַם (Dan. 4. 16) the Syriac forms having preformative אֶת may be compared.

12. Where OJ has *ē* in the final syllable (Pael, Aphel, Ithpᵉel) OTA sometimes has *ē* and sometimes *ī*. It is difficult to make a general statement on the subject, or to frame an accurate paradigm, because of the paucity of material. The following review includes all perfects, imperfects, imperatives, and participles of verbs other than those לא״ל (§ 27), which agree with OJ, and ע״י and ע״וע׳(§§ 32 and 34), which exhibit the vowels *ē* and *ī* in nearly equal proportion. In the PAEL perfect, examples of *ī* number four, against one of *ē* (Dan. 6. 1); in the imperf. and partic. there is one example of both on each side, of the imperat. no cases at all. In the HAPHEL the perfect (three examples) and the imperative (two examples) have *ē* (excluding הֵימִין, note 5), in the imperfect there are two cases of *ī* and two of *ē* (viz. תְּהוֹבֵד and תַּחַת), in the participle two cases of *ī*. In the HITHPᵉEL there are no cases of the perfect or imperative, in the imperfect there are four examples of *ī* and one of *ē*, and in the participle two examples of *ē*. The extent of the influence exercised by pause on these forms is very uncertain. For intransitive Pᵉal perfects see note 3.

§ 17. PERFECT TENSES

	PAEL.			PeAL.		
PTM	OJ	OJ	PTM	OJ		
	כַּתֵּיב	דְּסוּךְ		כְּתַב	3 s. m.
	כַּתֵּיבַת	דְּמוֹכַת		כְּתַבַת	f.
	כַּתֵּיבְתְּ -תָּא	דְּמוֹכְתְּ -תָּא		כְּתַבְתְּ -תָּא	2 s. m.
	כַּתֵּיבְתְּ	דְּמוֹכְתְּ		כְּתַבְתְּ	f.
	כַּתֵּיבִית	דְּמוֹכִית		כְּתַבִית	1 sing.
כַּתְּבוּן	כַּתֵּיבוּ	דְּמוֹכוּ	כַּתְבוּן	כְּתַבוּ	3 pl. m.
כַּתְּבָן	כַּתֵּיבָא	דְּמוֹכָא	כַּתְבָן	כְּתַבָא	f.
	כַּתֵּיבְתּוּן	דְּמוֹכְתּוּן		כְּתַבְתּוּן	2 pl. m.
	כַּתֵּיבְתִּין	דְּמוֹכְתִּין		כְּתַבְתִּין	f.
כַּתֵּיבְכְנַן	כַּתֵּיבְנָא	דְּמוֹכְנָא	כְּתַבְנַן	כְּתַבְנָא	1 plur.

Table. **1*.** The table represents the inflexion of all perfects, in ă, ĕ, and ū. The analogy of OTA (note 6) suggests that the supralinear 3 s. f. should be pronounced כְּתֵבַת rather than כְּתַבַת (§ 2. 6).

Endings. **2*.** The distinctive ending תָּא is more common in OJ than in PTM (Dalman) and is predominant in OTA (תְּ).

3*. The PTM plural endings *ūn* and *ān* are borrowed from the imperf. tense, to which they properly belong. *ū* and *ā* also occur in PTM.

4. In PTM יֵן .. occurs for וּן and יתוּן .. for תּוּן, especially in Aphels. The *ĕ* may have been transferred from the final syllable of the Aphel (Pael) stem. Dalman suggests the influence of the forms of § 21, note 7. Examples: אַפֵּקִינָן (25. 5), אַקְלִינָן (23. 9). The form אַתְקֵינָן (19. ii. 9) = אַתְקֵין + נָן.

Accent. **5*.** In OJ only the 2 plur. terminations are accented; in OTA the 2 plur., 3 s. f. (Syriac type—see note 6) and the 1 sing.; in PTM at least the 2 and 3 plur. terminations and possibly, like OTA, the 3 s. f. and 1 sing.

OTA. **6.** In OTA the 3 s. f. has two forms, one of the OJ type and the other resembling the Syriac form. The former occurs in two Peals (בְּטֵלַת, אֲמֵרַת) and in the few cases there are of Hithpeel (הִתְגְּזֵרַת) and Haphel (הַדְּקֵת) forms. The latter occurs in three Peals (סִלְקַת) and in two of three Hophals (הָחָרְבַת). In the Peal, Pael, and Hophal the 1 sing. has a form that resembles the Syriac (בְּרֵכֶת, יְדַעֵת). In the Haphel, besides הֲקֵימֵת (§ 33), only הַשְׁבַּחַת (Dan. 2. 25) occurs. The form resembles that of OJ and perhaps its vocalization, which is also that of a 3 s. f. perfect, should be הַשְׁבְּחַת (as הֲקֵימֵת) or הַשְׁבַּחַת (as in supralinear MSS.). The supralinear MSS. of OTA have a larger proportion of OJ forms than MT in the 3 s. f. perfect, but they do not wholly eliminate the Syriac type. The absence of vowels in the texts of PTM leaves it uncertain how far they agree with the forms of OJ and how far with those of OTA.

Syntax. **7.** In PTM the 2 pl. masc. form is always used for the 2 pl. fem. and frequently the 3 pl. m. for the 3 pl. f. (Dalman).

8. In PTM and OTA perfect tenses alternate with participles in narratives regarding the past (cf. § 21), and the use of successive sentences unconnected by conjunctions (asyndeton) is characteristic, especially of PTM. OJ follows the Hebrew text in its use of conjunctions. The perfect is used to express unfulfilled conditions after אִין (26. 18) and אִלּוּ (21. 11, 24. 1, 27. 12) and sometimes also as the tense of the following apodosis (21. 11), but not generally (see § 22, note 2 *f*).

§ 18. IMPERFECT TENSES

PAEL.—OJ AND PTM		PEAL.—OJ AND PTM		
PLUR.	SING.	PLUR.	SING.	
יְכַתְּבוּן	יְכַתֵּיב	יִכְתְּבוּן	יִכְתּוֹב	3 masc.
יְכַתְּבָן	תְּכַתֵּיב	יִכְתְּבָן	תִּכְתּוֹב	fem.
תְּכַתְּבוּן	תְּכַתֵּיב	תִּכְתְּבוּן	תִּכְתּוֹב	2 masc.
תְּכַתְּבָן	תְּכַתְּבִין	תִּכְתְּבָן	תִּכְתְּבִין	fem.
נְכַתֵּיב	אֲכַתֵּיב	נִכְתּוֹב	אִכְתּוֹב	1 m. and f.

Stem vowels. **1*.** The stem vowel of the imperf. Peal is rarely *ē*, except in the case of verbs final aleph or yodh (יֵעֵיד, יֵחֵוֵי, יִתֵּין). Pathaḥ is not usual in the imperff. Peal of intransitive verbs. For verbs final guttural see § 23. The occasional use of *ū* for *ō* and of *ī* for *ē* may originally have been limited to pausal forms, where it is found with special frequency (Deut. 16. 29).

2*. The stem vowels of other imperff. than the Peal agree with the corresponding vowels of the perfect. Examples: יִתְכְּנֵישׁ, יִשְׁפַּח, יִתְבְּחַר.

Preformative vowels. **3*.** Supralinear preformative pathaḥ (= seghol) in the 1 sing. imperf. Peal (as in Judg. 4. 7, 6. 15), except in the case of some verbs initial guttural (§ 23), is a usage of late Yemenite MSS. In OTA preformative seghol occurs twice in MT (אֶבְעֵא, אֶקְרֵא)[1] and ḥireq once (אִנְדַּע).

4*. In the supralinear MSS. published by Kahle the preformative vowel of the 1 sing. imperf. Pael is regularly אֱ, and אַ is commonly written in the unvocalized texts of PTM. This orthography is to be regarded as a representation of ḥateph seghol (§ 2. 8). אֶסָּעֲרֵם in the MT of Zech. 7. 14 may be compared. The only 1 sing. imperf. Pael form in OTA is אֲחַוֵּא (Dan. 2. 24).

5. After the final consonant of the preformative syllables of the imperff. Peal and Aphel an intrusive vowel (ḥireq) is sometimes indicated by the supralinear punctuation (e. g. יִשְׁלְטוּן = יִשְׁלְטֻן, Deut. 15. 6—Kahle p. 222). So also in the Ithpeel (§ 16, note 8).

Prefix ל.   6. Forms of 3 s. m. imperf. with preformative ל (Brockelmann, *Grundriss*, i. 565) are found in PTM (21. ii. 6). Examples: לְפֵּיק, לְמוּת, לֵיכוּל, לְהֱוֵי) לִיפַק, לִימוּת, לֵיכוּל, לְהוּי). They seem to occur generally in certain special types of sentence, e. g. in those expressing a purpose (after דְּ and דִּלָא) or a wish (see Dalman, p. 264 f.). In OTA the forms לֶהֱוֵא (לֶהֱוֵה), לֶהֱוֹן, and לֶהֱוְיָן occur. They may have been preferred in order to avoid the use of forms resembling the divine name יהוה.

OTA.   7. In OTA the stem vowels of the imperf. Peal are *ū* (יִסְגֻּד), *ă* (יִלְבַּשׁ), and *ĕ* (יִפֵּל) and those of the impff. Pael and Haphel *ē* or *ī* (§ 16, note 12). In the Haphel imperf. uncontracted forms are nearly always used (יְהַשְׁבַּח, יְהַשְׁפִּל). The plural ending *ū* (or *ō*), for *ūn*, occurs twice (§ 29, note 10; § 35, note 5). See also notes 3, 4 and 6.

Syntax.   8. In PTM the uses of the imperfect tense are very strictly limited:

(1) It is a jussive (21. ii. 6, 26. 17, 27. 6) or imperative (with negative, 16. ii. 4, 19. ii. 7 f., 22. ii. 5 ; as a polite imperat., 24. ii. 7)

---

[1] In the supralinear MSS. probably ḥireq, as Dan. 5. 17 (Strack).

and expresses wishes, imprecations (26, last line, 28, second last line) and resolves (18. 9, 28. 6—see (4) below).

(2) It is used after דְּ and דְּלָא to express purpose (18. 13, 18. ii. 4, 21. 15), after דְּלָא = lest (24. 3) and after ד (or דלא) in dependence upon verbs of asking (21. 2) and ordering (23. 5).

(3) It is used modally (21. 3), especially in questions (19. ii. 9, 20. ii. 7, 24. ii. 2, 25. ii. 8). Cf. note 9 (3).

(4) It is a future tense only when there is an implication of indefiniteness (19. iii. 3 'that I should go out', 22. 1 'should be married', 28. 6, כָּל דְּיֵימַר לִי בַּר נָשָׁא אֶעֱבֵיד 'everything that any one *may bid me* I will do'), in subordinate clauses.

9. In OJ the imperfect tense is used more extensively than in PTM. It is employed:

(1) As an imperative, jussive, and voluntative, expressing commands and exhortations (Gen. 6. 21, Exod. 22. 24, Deut. 16. 18, Josh. 23. 8, 13, 1 Sam. 24. 13), and resolves (Gen. 6. 7, Josh. 24.15, 1 Sam. 24. 11).

(2) After בְּדִיל דְּ in purpose clauses (Gen. 12. 13, 27. 25, Exod. 8. 6, 11. 7, Deut. 4. 1, 5. 16, 8. 1, 11. 8).

(3) As the usual equivalent of most Hebrew modal imperfects (to be rendered by may, might, would, should, must, &c.). 'Could' is expressed by an imperfect (2 Sam. 2. 22, 1 Kings 8. 5) or a participle (1 Kings 18. 10, Jer. 24. 2), or by אֶפְשָׁר דְּ with an imperf. (Gen. 13. 16). 'Can' may also be expressed by אֶפְשָׁר דְּ (Isai. 49. 15).

(4) As the ordinary future tense, for which PTM uses the participle. Examples: Gen. 2. 17, 3. 4, 49. 1, Exod. 4. 1, 6. 1, Deut. 16. 18, Josh. 1. 3, 18, 3. 5, 10, 13, 18. 8, 23. 5, 1 Sam. 24. 21.

(5) In conditional sentences, following אִם (Gen. 18. 26, Exod. 22. 24, Josh. 23. 12) and אֲרֵי (Hebrew כִּי), Josh. 24. 20. A participle, however, is used to translate a Hebrew participle (Gen. 43. 4 f.).

(6) As a future in the past (preterite future)—Gen. 2. 19, Exod. 2. 4, 1 Sam. 22. 22, 2 Kings 13. 14—for which a participle (Gen. 43. 25, 1 Kings 7. 7) or עֲתִיד דְּ with an imperf. (2 Kings 3. 27) are possible alternatives.

10. In OTA the imperfect is used as the ordinary future tense, as a jussive, and in the various modal senses. It is also used in conditional sentences, referring to the future (English indefinite present). It seldom refers to the present or the past.

11. עֲתִיד ('ready', 'prepared') or עֲתִיד לְ, with an infinitive, also expresses future time in OJ and PTM (Gen. 4. 10, 41. 28, Exod. 16. 23; Dalman, *Grammar*, p. 268 f.).

12. Sometimes an imperfect tense depends directly upon a governing verb, without דְּ (§ 7, note 7) being prefixed (29. 21, רַבָּנָן הָכָא בָּעַן נִיצַלֵּי וְיֵיחוֹת מִטְרָא 'Our teachers here ask (that) I should pray, so that rain may fall'). Cf. כָּל סַמָּא דְמִלְּתָא נִפּוֹק לִי מִן הָכָא (19. iii. 3) 'the only remedy of the affair is that I should go out from here'. For ניצלי and נפוק see note 13.

13. In PTM the 1 plur. imperf. is often used for the 1 sing. impf. (19. iii. 3, 21. 1, 24. ii. 7, 29. 21; Dalman, p. 265 f.). Cf. Dan. 2. 36, and see § 21, note 14.

§ 19. IMPERATIVES

PAEL.		PᵉAL.		OJ	
כַּתֵּיב	מְנַע	עֲבֵיד	כְּתוֹב		2 s. m.
כַּתֵּיבִי	מְנַעִי	עֲבִידִי	כְּתוּבִי		f.
כַּתֵּיבוּ	מְנַעוּ	עֲבִידוּ	כְּתוּבוּ		2 pl. m.
כַּתֵּיבָא	מְנַעָא	עֲבִידָא	כְּתוּבָא		f.
					PTM
כַּתֵּיב	מְנַע	עֲבֵיד	כְּתוֹב		2 s. m.
כַּתְּבִין	מַנְעִין	עַבְדִין	כּוּתְבִין		f.
כַּתְּבוּן	מַנְעוּן	עַבְדוּן	כּוּתְבוּן		2 pl. m.
כַּתְּבֶן	מַנְעֶן	עַבְדֶן	כּוּתְבֶן		f.

1*. In PTM the terminations are accented, in OJ unaccented.

2*. The final stem vowel of an imperative form agrees generally with that of the corresponding imperfect tense (cf. § 18, note 1).

3*. The MSS. of PTM indicate only *u* as the stem vowel of the inflected forms of the P^eal imperatives. *ĭ* was probably in some cases the stem vowel, as well as *ă* (see § 25, note 5, and § 36, note 9). עֲבְדִין might have been given as the paradigm form.

4*. In OJ and PTM the plural imperative of the derived stems is the same as their 3 plur. perf. and in some verbs the plural imperat. P^eal is also ambiguous (מַנְעוּן, מְנַעוּ).

5. ἐφφαθά is understood by Dalman (p. 278, note 1) to be 2 plur. fem. imperative Ethp^eel, having ת assimilated to פ (§ 16, note 7) and with the fem. plur. ending silent as in Syriac, the man's *ears* being addressed (in Dalman 'Augen' should be 'Ohren'). Accordingly אֶתְפְּתַחָא = אֶפְּתַח = ἐφφαθά (ה not being distinguished from א in Galilee—Dalman, p. 57 f.).

OTA. **6.** OTA imperatives agree in terminations and accentuation with the imperatives of OJ. The OTA forms corresponding to כְּתוֹב and אַכְתֵּיב are כְּתַב (one example) and הַכְתֵּב (two examples).

§ 20. INFINITIVES

BAB	PTM	OJ	OJ	
	מִכְתַּב		מִכְתַּב	P^eal
	מִכְתּוֹב			
	מִכְתְּבָא			
כַּתּוֹבֵי	מְכַתְּבָא	כַּתָּבוּת	כַּתָּבָא	Pael
אַכְתּוֹבֵי	מַכְתְּבָא	אַכְתָּבוּת	אַכְתָּבָא	Aphel
אִתְכְּתוֹבֵי	מִתְכְּתָבָא	אִתְכְּתָבוּת	אִתְכְּתָבָא	Ithp^eel
אִתְכַּתּוֹבֵי	מִתְכַּתְּבָא	אִתְכַּתָּבוּת	אִתְכַּתְּבָא	Ithpaal
	מִתַּכְתְּבָא	אִתַּכְתָּבוּת	אִתַּכְתְּבָא	Ittaphal

Orthography.   1*. The feminine ending of the infinitives
of the derived stems in PTM is often represented by ה, and this
orthography is usual in OTA.

BAB.   2. The forms under BAB, which are of Babylonian
origin, occur occasionally in OJ (Judg. 3. 26) and PTM (23. 3).

OJ.   3*. The OJ forms in *ūth* are used in the construct and
with suffixes.   Penultimate *ā* is unchangeable (קַדְמוּתֵיהּ, Gen.
14. 17).

PTM.   4*. The infinn. of the derived stems in PTM are inflected like feminine nouns (מַפְּקָתְהוֹן, 16. ii. 8—infin. Aphel of
נְפַק).

OTA.   5. In OTA the forms are generally those of OJ, but
with preformative ה for א (see paradigm, p. 95).   הַנְוָקַת (Ezra 4. 22),
with construct ending as in PTM, is exceptional.

Infin. Pᵉal.   6*. In OJ and OTA infinn. Pᵉal are inflected as
nouns of the B class מִקְרְבִי, מִקָרַבְהוֹן (§ 12, note 5).   In PTM the
termination בּ–ִ (§ 36, note 8) is added to the Pᵉal infinitive before
suffixes (מִקְרְבֵּיהּ).

Syntax.   7. The adverbial use of the Hebrew infin. absolute
(as in Deut. 15. 4, 5, 8) is exactly reproduced by OJ, and the Pᵉal
infinitive form is then generally written מִכְתַּב in the supralinear
MSS. (but cf. מִזְבַּן in 2 Sam. 24. 24, Kahle, p. 28).   The idiom is
infrequent in PTM (Dalman, p. 280).

8. In OJ an infinitive dependent on a governing verb is nearly
always preceded by לֹ, even when there is no preposition in the
Hebrew text (Exod. 2. 3, Deut. 1. 19, 2. 25, Num. 22. 14, Judg.
8. 3, Isai. 1. 14).   In OTA the use of לֹ is invariable.   In PTM
both constructions occur, with לֹ (19. ii. 11, 20. ii. 1 and 3, 22. ii. 6,
24. ii. 1 and 4, 26. 10), and without לֹ (19. ii. 10, 27. 2, 3, 6 and 8,
29. 7).

9. A Hebrew infinitive in the nominative case is generally
replaced in OJ by לֹ with an imperfect (Gen. 2. 18, 29. 19, Exod.

14. 12, Judg. 18. 19), or a perfect (Gen. 30. 15), or a partic. (Isai.
7. 13). Examples of the retention of the infin. occur in 1 Sam.
15. 22, 29. 6, Isai. 10. 7.

10. The Hebrew negative לְבִלְתִּי is represented in OJ by בְּדִיל
דְּלָא לְ (with an infin.), e.g. in Gen. 3. 11, 4. 15, Deut. 4. 21, 8. 11,
Josh. 5. 6, Judg. 2. 23. In OTA לָא לְ with an infin. means 'must
not be'.

11. A peculiarity of the syntax of OTA is that a single object
noun, with no qualification, stands before a governing infin. (Dan.
3. 16, 5. 16, &c.). Cf. Dan. 2. 12, 3. 19, 5. 7, 7. 25, where the
object follows. Objects such as generally follow a governing infin.
may also precede the infin. (Dan. 2. 10, 3. 32, 5. 15, &c.) and do so
freely in Ezra (4. 14, 5. 13, &c.).

§ 21. PARTICIPLES

APHEL.	PAEL.		PEAL.	
	PTM	OJ		
מַכְתֵּיב	מְכַתֵּיב	מְכַתֵּיב	כָּתֵיב	active
מַכְתַּב	מְכַתַּב	מְכוּתַּב	כְּתִיב	passive

ITTAPHAL.	ITHPAAL.	ITHPᵉEL.
מִתַּכְתַּב	מִתְכַּתַּב	מִתְכְּתֵיב

Forms. **1*.** Since verbs final guttural and resh have ă for ē
in all final syllables אָמַר is the partic. Peal of אֲמַר, and there is no
distinction between the active and passive forms of the Pael and
Aphel participles of such verbs. On the other hand, מְשֵׁיזֵיב (Deut.
3. 3, Judg. 12. 5) and מְשֵׁתֵיזֵיב (from שֵׁיזֵיב, rescue) are passives as
well as actives.

2*. In OJ ī sometimes appears for final ē (so עָבִיד in 1 Kings
1. 6, Kahle, p. 28, and מְרַחִים in Deut. 28. 50, Kahle, p. 225).

Peal particc. used as nouns always have *ī* in the supralinear punctuation (so פָּרִיק, סָהִיד, כָּהִין). In OTA *ē* is usual, but eight words have *ī* for *ē*, viz.:

יְכָל, נָחַת, דָּלַק, נָזַק, מְמַלֵּל, מַשְׁפֵּל, מַצַּל, מְשֵׁיזִב.

3*. The particc. of intrans. verbs have the same forms as those of trans. verbs. Examples: דָּמֵיךְ (also דָּמוּךְ) 'sleeping'; רָחֵיץ (also רְחִיץ) 'trusting', 'hoping'; דָּחֵיל (also דָּחוּל) 'fearing'.

4*. Words of the form כְּתִיב may have an active sense. Examples: סָבִיר 'thinking'; דְּכִיר 'remembering'; תְּמֵיהַּ (? also תָּמֵיהַּ) 'wondering'.

5. The form מְכוּתַּב occurs occasionally in PTM and מְכַתַּב (especially with verbs medial guttural) in OJ (Gen. 2. 9).

Inflexions. **6.** Participles are inflected like nouns of the B class (§ 10, note 7). There is, therefore, no formal distinction between active and passive in the particc. Pael and Aphel when these are inflected (מְכַתְּבָא, &c.). Forms like תמיהין (17. ii. 18), מקילין (23. 8), יתיבא (27. 2), and עבידא (28. 17) occur in the unvocalized texts of PTM and are read by Dalman as עֲבֵידָא, &c. They do not occur in MSS. having a supralinear vocalization (Dalman, p. 311). Possibly yodh in such cases signifies vocal shewa (§ 2. 8).

7*. Shortened forms of the personal pronouns of the first and second persons (נָא, אֲנַ, תְּ, and תּוּן) joined to particc. make a new tense form. Examples: יָדַעְנָא (Gen. 4. 9), רָכְבַּתְּ (Berliner) or רָכֵיבְתְּ (Merx), in Num. 22. 30, זָרַעַתְּ (Deut. 11. 10, Kahle, p. 16), יָדְעִינַן (25. ii. 8),[1] יָדַעְתּוּן (Judg. 5. 16). See also § 30, note 5.

8. Tense forms got by uniting particc. and perf. terminations also occur, e.g. מְצַלַּן (or מְצַלּוֹן, § 28, note 1), meaning 'they prayed' (Dalman, p. 284).

---

[1] So Dalman (cf. *Gram.*, p. 290); why not יָדְעִינַן?

Syntax. **9.** In PTM participles take over much of the early usage of imperfect tenses. They serve as an ordinary future tense (15. 9, 16. 5—יְתֵיב, 20. 11, 23. ii. 8, 26. 3), and as the English indefinite present (= future) in conditional sentences (16. ii. 13), and they express promises (15. 10, 20. ii. 11) and general truths (23. 8). With עַד 'while' (14. ii. 4), and in an object sentence dependent on a past tense (16. ii. 11) they are used as past progressives and may sometimes be rendered by an English past tense (24. 2). The use of particc. in place of perfect tenses in narratives of past events is very characteristic (24. ii. 3, 25. ii. 2 ff., 27. 9—אָמְרָה).

10. In OJ particc. often represent Hebrew imperff. (or consecutive perff.), but not to the same extent as in PTM and not in the same uses. Acts customary in the present (Exod. 18. 15, Num. 11. 12, Deut. 1. 31 and 44, Judg. 7. 5, 10. 4, 1 Sam. 5. 5, 16. 7, 2 Kings 9. 20) or in the past (Gen. 29. 2, Num. 9. 20, Judg. 2. 19, 6. 5, 14. 10, 1 Sam. 1. 3, 6, 7, 2. 13 f. and 19) are expressed by particc. For the different idiom employed by PTM, see § 22, note 2 (c).

In questions understood of present time, a Hebrew imperf. is rendered in OJ by a participle (Gen. 32. 29 = 32. 30, 37. 15, Exod. 2. 13, 3. 3, Judg. 17. 9, 19. 17, 1 Sam. 1. 8, 25. 10, 28. 16).[1]

So, also, when the Hebrew imperf. denotes continuance of a state through a period in the past (Gen. 2. 25, Exod. 13. 22, 1 Sam. 1. 13, Isai. 10. 7) or the future (1 Sam. 1. 14).

11. In OTA the partic. is the ordinary equivalent of a present tense (Dan. 2. 8) and a very frequent alternative to a perfect in narratives of past events (Dan. 4. 4, Ezra 5. 3). It is also used as a progressive tense, descriptive of events in the present (Dan. 3. 25—מְהַלְכִין) or the past (Dan. 5. 5—כָּתְבָה), and in stating general

---

[1] In OJ an imperfect in questions is to be understood as a future (Gen. 16.8), or in a modal sense (Gen. 27. 45, 1 Sam. 17. 8, 28. 15). Cf. § 18, note 9.

truths (Dan. 2. 21). Occasionally it alternates with the imperfect as a future tense (Dan. 4. 29).

12. When the pronoun subject of a partic. is in the third person, it is often left unexpressed (*Chrest.* 15. 11, 16. ii. 3, 20. 8, 24. 10, 27. 9; Dan. 4. 4, 4. 32).

13. A general statement with an indefinite subject is expressed by the plural of a partic. without an explicit subject. Examples: *Chrest.* 27. 11, 'men despise'; Ezra 6. 3, 'men sacrifice'; Dan. 4. 28, equivalent to a passive 'you are addressed'.

14. The 1 pers. plur. of the participle tense (note 7) may be used for the 1 pers. sing. (Dalman, p. 266). Cf. § 18, note 13.

15. Some verbs take as their complement a participle, instead of an infin. Examples: קוּם (14. ii. 1), שָׁרִי (16. ii. 9, 20. 10), עֲבַד (19. 13). שרי ('begin') is used with particc. in the Peshitta, but with infinn. in OJ (Gen. 6. 1, Deut. 2. 31, Judg. 10. 18, 13. 5, 1 Sam. 14. 35) and in OTA (Ezra 5. 2).

§ 22. COMPOUND TENSES

1*. The tenses of the verb הֲוָה 'become' form compound tenses with the participles of other verbs. These compound tenses occur frequently in PTM and are also a characteristic feature of OTA. They are seldom used by OJ.

2. In PTM the perfect of הֲוָה joined to a present participle expresses:

(*a*) *A past progressive tense*, in sentences introduced by 'who' or 'when' (14. ii. 1, 15. ii. 1, 22. 7) and in circumstantial clauses (15. 6, 16. ii. 5). It describes a prolonged state or act in the past, where in English a past tense is a possible (22. 3, 27. ii. 1) or a preferable (16. ii. 5, 16. ii. 8) alternative. The verbs employed are very frequently intrans. verbs denoting state or condition. Examples: כַּד הֲוָה אָתֵי 'when he was coming', וְהוּא הֲוָה יָדַע 'now he

knew'. In the sentence וַהֲוָת בָּכְיָה גּוֹ אִסְטְרָטָה וַאֲמָרִית לַהּ מָה לִיךְ
(29. 6) the compound tense possibly expresses a past inchoative,
'when she began weeping in the street, I asked her what was the
matter'.

(*b*) *A pluperfect progressive tense*, in sentences dependent on a past
tense (16. 6, 'he found that he had been selling').

(*c*) *A habit or custom*, in the present (21. 12) or the past (22. ii. 2,
23. ii. 7, 27. 1, 28. 6, 'he used to say').

(*d*) *An act repeated in the past* a number of times, by the same or
by different persons (15. 3, 19, ii. 15—כָּל מַאן דַּהֲוָה אָתֵי לְתַמָּן הֲוָה
עָבֵיד כֵּן—21. 13, 22. 7).

(*e*) *A future in the past* (preterite future), 'he lay down beside
one of them in order to learn what they would say' (17. ii. 4 f.).

(*f*) *A past conditional*, expressing 'would have' (22. 9, after הֵיךְ,
24. 2, 27. 12, both in apodoses of conditional sentences, after unfulfilled conditions).

3. The participle tense of הֲוָה (see § 21, note 7) may be used,
instead of its perfect tense, in combination with the present participle of another verb. Examples: הֲוֵינָא מְגַלֵּיא 'I repeatedly un-
covered' (22. 7), מָה הֲוֵינָה מְסָעַר דַּעְתִּי 'How could I have diverted
my attention?' (29. 28). For the expression of 'could have' by a
compound tense see also note 5.

4. In OTA the uses of the perfect compound tense, so far as
they occur, are the same as in PTM. Examples: (*a*) Dan. 2. 31,
5. 19—הֲוֹ וָזְעִין 'trembled', describing a prolonged state or condition; (*c*) Dan. 5. 19—הֲוָה קָטֵל 'he used to kill'; (*d*) Dan. 6. 11,
three times in the day he knelt on his knees and prayed' (הֲוָא בָּרֵךְ
וּמְצַלֵּא . . .) and Dan. 6. 5, 'they sought repeatedly to find an
excuse' (הֲוֹ בָעַיִן). In Dan. 6. 15 הֲוָה מִשְׁתַּדַּר may be classed under
(*a*) or (*d*).

5*. In OJ a participle or an imperfect tense is generally used
where PTM would use a compound perfect tense. A compound

perfect is, however, sometimes used to describe an act or state
extending over a period of time (Gen. 2. 6, 19, Josh. 4. 14, 'as
they had reverenced') or repeated at intervals during a period of
time (Gen. 31. 18). It is also used in the apodosis of conditional sentences (Judg. 11. 39, 'he would have redeemed') and to
express 'could have' (Gen. 43. 7). It is of course the regular
equivalent of the same compound tense in Hebrew (Gen. 4. 17,
37. 2, &c.).

6*. The imperfect יְהֵא joined to the present participle of another
verb is used (*a*) as a future progressive tense (Exod. 1. 16, after כַּד),
(*b*) to express future custom or habit (Dan. 2. 43), and (*c*) after וְ
and דְּלָא to express result or effect (*Chrest.* 16. ii. 14, 18. 15, 20. 5 ;
Dan. 6. 3, Ezra 6. 10, 7. 25 f.) or the substance of a command
(22. ii. 3 f.). As an alternative to a simple jussive this tense perhaps
implies emphasis or menace (*Chrest.* 19. ii. 17 ; cf. Ezra 6. 8 f.).
For corresponding uses of the imperfect see § 18, note 8 (2).

7. A relative sentence contains a compound tense when there is
a compound tense in the associated principal clause (Dan. 5. 19—
דִּי הֲוָא צָבֵא—Ezra 7. 26, *Chrest.* 19. ii. 15).

8*. הֲוָה joined to a passive participle provides the equivalent of
a simple perfect passive (17. ii. 2, 25. ii. 10; Dan. 6. 4, Ezra 5. 11).
יְהֵא with a passive participle is used as a jussive passive (Dan. 3. 18,
Ezra 4. 12, 6. 8 f.); cf. note 6.

9. In PTM, as in Syriac, the perfect of any verb may be
slightly strengthened by prefixing to it the perfect of הֲוָה (Dalman,
p. 257 f.).

10. אֲתָא in combination with an infinitive is sometimes equivalent to a compound tense (20. ii. 10—מִדְּאָתֵי א׳ מִכְבּוֹשׁ מְדִינְתָּא 'after
(he) had conquered the city'.

§ 23. INFLUENCE OF GUTTURALS UPON VERBAL FORMS

The influence of gutturals (ה, ח, ע) and of ר upon the vowels of verbal forms is not as extensive as in Hebrew, but, so far as it goes, is similar in character.

1*. Pathaḥ holds the place of normal ṣere in the final syllable of all parts of verbs final guttural or resh (Pael, Aphel, partic. Peal, &c.). In the final syllable of imperff. and imperatives Peal pathaḥ is usual, but $\bar{o}$ also occurs before final resh and final 'ayin, especially in PTM. In OTA pathaḥ is used in all the cases covered by this section. The verbs of §§ 27, 32, and 34 are not included.

2*. In the imperf. Peal **preformative pathaḥ** is used in some verbs (e.g. יַחְבֻּט, יֶעְשׂוֹק, יַעֲבִיד), but ḥireq is more common (Dalman). In OTA תַּעַבְדוּן (twice), יַחְלְפוּן (once) and יֶעְדֵּה or תֶּעְדֵּא (thrice), with the imperfect forms of הֲוָה (תֶּהֱוֵא, &c.), are the only Peal imperff. of verbs initial guttural that occur. Dalman (page 93) makes the supralinear pathaḥ of יַעֲבִיד equivalent to seghol (hence *Chrest.* 18. 4, 19. ii. 9, 20. ii. 7).

3*. Apparently the only **infin. with preformative pathaḥ** is מַעֲבַד. In OTA the form is מֶעְבַּד (twice) and Dalman follows this analogy in his *Dialektproben* (18. 14, 29. 7).

4*. Pathaḥ furtive is used in the pass. partic. Peal of verbs final guttural (שְׁלִיחַ). See also § 32, note 1.

5*. An **intrusive pathaḥ** separates the termination תְּ from the stem of verbs final guttural. E. g. הִשְׁתְּכַחַתְּ (Dan. 5. 27).

6*. Vocal shewa following a guttural in the supralinear punctuation is to be pronounced as the sublinear ḥateph would be. Supralinear pathaḥ in perff. like אֲמַר signifies **ḥateph pathaḥ** and ṣere in imperative forms like אֵימַר and עֵיבַר signifies **ḥateph seghol.** See § 2. 7, 8.

7*. An **intrusive ḥateph** (before vocal shewa an intrusive pathaḥ) is indicated in some MSS. of OJ after initial ע and initial ח in the imperf. and infin. forms of the Peal (Aphel, Shaphel). יַעֲבֵיד and מַעֲבַד are most frequently so treated. Cf. Judg. 12. 5 (אֶעֱבָר) and 16. 24 (מַחֲרִיב, Hebraism?). In some MSS. after ע an **intrusive ḥireq** is indicated, in harmony with the ḥireq of the preformative syllable (Dalman, p. 93; Kahle, p. 223). For forms with intrusive vowels in OTA see note 2.

8*. In the intensives of verbs medial resh, in which the medial radical is not doubled, the preceding pathaḥ is regularly lengthened into **compensation qameṣ** and, similarly, sometimes before medial ע or א. Examples: סָאֵיב, גְּעֵיל, בָּרֵיךְ. In Dan. 5. 9 the sublinear reading is מְתְבְּהַל and the supralinear is מִתְבַּהַל (or מִתְבְּהַל).

9. א between two vowels was pronounced yodh (Dalman, p. 60), hence PTM in the inflected forms of the active partic. Peal of verbs medial aleph and in the intensive forms of שְׁאֵיל and שְׁאַר writes י for א. PTM שְׁיֵיל and שַׁיַּר = OJ שְׁאֵיל (Gen. 43. 7—Dalman, p. 305) and שְׁאַר. See also § 33, note 2.

§ 24. VERBS INITIAL NUN

נְחַת	סְלֵק, סְלֵיק	נְסַב, נְסֵיב	נְפַק	Peal	perf.
יֵיחוֹת	יִסַּק	יִסַּב	יִפּוֹק		imperf.
חוֹת	סַק	סַב	פּוֹק		imperat.
חוֹתוּ	סָקוּ	סַבוּ	פּוּקוּ		
מֵיחַת	מִסַּק	מִסַּב	מִפַּק		infin.
מֵיחוֹת	מִסּוֹק	מִסּוֹב	מִפּוֹק		PTM
נָחֵית	סָלֵיק	נָסֵיב	נָפֵיק		partic.
אַחֵית	אַפֵּיק		אַפֵּיק	Aphel	perf.
יַחֵית	יַפֵּיק		יַפֵּיק		imperf.
אַחֵית	אַפֵּיק		אַפֵּיק		imperat.
אַחְתָּא	אַפְקָא		אַפְקָא		infin.
מַחֵית	מַפֵּיק		מַפֵּיק		partic.

Assimilation.   **1*.** Assimilation of nun to the medial radical takes place in the impff. and inff. Peal and in all the tenses of the Aphel and Ittaphal. Nun and its vowel (shewa) generally disappear in the imperat. Peal.

2*. In verbs medial ה and medial ע assimilation of nun does not take place (Gen. 1. 17, אַנְהְרָא). Unassimilated forms of other verbs also occur (22. ii. 9, יִנְזוֹף; Gen. 26.11, יִנְזִיק).

3*. The vocalization of verbs medial ח, according to the supralinear punctuation, is shown above. Where pathah is written in the perfect Aphel (Gen. 2. 5, Merx), it may be understood to denote hateph pathaḥ (§ 2. 7).

Peal imperatt. and infinn.   **4*.** The stem vowels of the imperative Peal do not become vocal shewa in the inflected forms, as they do in Hebrew (see table above). Forms with nun preserved sometimes occur in PTM. סִיב (15.9, 16. ii. 7) is an alternative to סַב.

5. Infinitives like מִפַּק are normal in OJ, and those like מִפּוֹק in PTM.

Ithpᵉel.   **6.** Ithpᵉel forms sometimes assimilate ת of the prefix to the following nun (§ 16, note 7).

7*. סליק In סליק *l* assimilates regressively, so that forms like those of verbs initial nun are produced. The infin. Haphel הַנְסָקָה (Dan. 6. 24) is a case of erroneous dissimilation (cf. § 10, note 12).

OTA.   **8.** So far as examples occur, notes 1–4 apply to OTA. The only verb medial guttural is נְחַת, whose nun is assimilated in the Haphel imperfect (תַּחַת), imperative (Ezra 5. 15, אֲחֵת or אַחֵת) and partic. (מְהַחֲתִין), but not in the Hophal (הָנְחַת). Other verbs with unassimilated forms are נתן (imperf., inf.), נפק (Aphel), and נזק (Aphel). There are two *ē* imperfects, יִפֵּל (as Syriac; OJ יִפּוֹל) and יָנְתֵּן or יִנְתֵּן. For the imperat. שָׂא see § 27, note 10, and for סְלֵק, note 7.

§ 25. VERBS INITIAL ALEPH

APHEL.		PEAL.		
אוֹבֵיד	אֲזַל	אֲמַר	אֲכַל	perf.
יוֹבֵיד	יֵיזֵיל	יֵימַר	יֵיכוֹל	imperf.
אוֹבֵיד	אִיזֵיל, אִיזֵיל	אֵימַר	אֵיכוֹל	imperat.
אוֹבִידוּ	אִיזִילוּ	אֵימַרוּ	אֵיכוּלוּ	OJ
אוֹבְדוּן	אֶזְלוּן	אִמְרוּן	אִכְלוּן	PTM
אוֹבָדָא	מֵיזַל	מֵימַר	מֵיכַל	infin.
מוֹבֵיד	אָזֵיל	אָמַר	אָכֵיל	partic.

1*. In the imperf. and infin. Peal and in the Aphel א coalesces with the preformative vowel into *ē* and *ō* respectively, and the orthography is generally the same as that of verbs initial yodh (אוֹבֵיד, יֵיכוֹל).

Peal imperf. 2*. The imperfects Peal, that have pathaḥ as their stem vowel, are יֵילַף, יֵיבַד, יֵימַר, and יֵיסַר (but also יֵיסוֹר). The final stem vowel of the imperatives of these words is also pathaḥ (in Hebrew holem). יֵיכוֹל does not belong to the group (unlike Hebrew יֹאכַל).

Imperat. 3*. The supralinear imperatives אֵיכוֹל, אֵימַר, &c., although pointed with ṣere, should probably be pronounced אֱמַר, אֱכוֹל, &c. (§ 2. 8), as in OTA (אֱמַר). In the supralinear MSS. of OJ אִיזֵיל (Exod. 33. 1, Deut. 10. 11—Kahle, pp. 5 and 15) and אִיזֵיל (Judg. 18. 19—Praetorius) both occur, and the plural form is אִיזֵילוּ (Josh. 2. 1, 18. 8). In the singular Berliner's *Onkelos* has both *ē* (Deut. 10. 11) and *ī* (Gen. 22. 2, Exod. 3. 16, 33. 1). In all these forms yodh presumably at first represented a hurried vowel (vocal shewa).

4*. Some verbs (e.g. אתא, אזל) use shortened imperatt. Peal as alternatives to the full forms (זֵיל, זֵילוּ; תָּא, תּוּ—in Dalman זֵיל). For the ending *ō* in תּוּ see § 29.

5*. The stem vowel *i* of the imperat. plur. of PTM is indicated
in the texts for some words and may have been the stem vowel of
all words of this class. The analogy of the imperat. sing. with
suffixes points to *i* or *u* (§ 36, note 9). Dalman's pointing אָזְלוּן
and אֲכְלוּן (23. 1) seems unlikely.

Aphel. **6*.** Of the Aphels with preformative ṣere that occur in
PTM only אֵיכִיל, הֵימִין and some verbs having both initial א and
final א, such as אתא, are recognized by Dalman (p. 298 f.) as correct.
The salutation אַיְשַׁר 'hail' (*Chrest.* 29. 19) is also supposed to be
an Aphel form (imperative). In OJ and OTA הימין (§ 16, note 5)
and אִיתִי or אֵיתִי (OTA הֵיתִי, הַיְתִי), from אֲתָא, are used.

Contracted forms. **7.** Contraction takes place in the imperf.,
infin., and partic. of אלף (מַלָּפָא, יַלֵּיף, יָאֵלֵּיף = מַלֵּיף, &c.). Contracted
Ithpᵉels and Ithpaals also occur (e.g. אתאֲמַר = אִתְּמַר and אִתַּחַד
= אִתְאֲחַד. There seems to be similar contraction of verbs initial
yodh (in אתיליד, Gen. 4. 18, 26, 24. 15, Merx).

Unusual forms. **8.** יבד and ילף (18. ii. 2) are used as alternative forms of אבד and אלף (cf. § 23, note 9). יֵימָא (= יֵימַר) is a
Babylonian form, which occurs in PTM (16. 5). אֲכֵילְנַן (17. ii. 7)
seems to have no parallel and may be an error for אכלינן (§ 21,
note 7) or אֲכֵילְנָא.

OTA. **9.** The variations of OTA are as follows. Etymo-
logical aleph is generally written in the Pᵉal imperf. and infin.
(מֵאמַר, יֵאכֻל), except in the cases of מֵתא and מֵזא, from אתא and
אזא (§ 27). In the Pᵉal imperat. א is generally followed by ḥateph
seghol and in אֱכֻל־ (Ezra 5. 15) ṣere is its equivalent (cf. note 3 and
אֱזֵה, Dan. 3. 22, = אֱזֵה, pass. ptc. Pᵉal). In Dan. 7. 5, where MT
has אֲכֻלִי, Strack's supralinear text reads אָכְלִי, i.e. אֲכֻלִי (§ 2. 8, 9)
The Hophal. perf. הוּבַד (Dan. 7. 11) has the same form as the
Hophal of verbs initial yodh. See also note 6 and the table of
verbs, p. 96.

§ 26. VERBS INITIAL YODH AND WAW

APHEL.				PEAL.	
אוֹטֵיב	יְרַת	יְתַב	יְדַע	יְכֵיל	perf.
	יְרִית	יְתֵיב			
יוֹטֵיב	יֵירַת	יִתֵּיב	יִדַּע	יִכּוֹל	imperf.
אוֹטֵיב	רַת	תֵּיב	דַּע	—	imperat.
אוֹטֵיבוּ	רַתוּ	תִּיבוּ	דְּעוּ		
אוֹטָבָא		מִתַּב	מִדַּע	מִכַּל	infin.
	מֵירַת	מֵיתַב	מֵידַע	מֵיכַל	

Peal prefixes. 1*. In the imperf. and infin. Peal yodh coalesces with the preformative vowel into (1) $\bar{e}$ and (2) $\check{i}$ followed by the middle radical doubled. In the imperf. tense $\bar{e}$ is unusual except before a medial guttural or resh (יֵירַת, יֵיהַב) and the punctuation of the MSS. cannot always be relied on. Examples: תֵּיבַשׁ (Ezek. 17. 10—Kahle, p. 46), יֵימַב (Deut. 10. 13—Kahle, p. 15; Ezra 7. 18), נֵיכוֹל (Josh. 9. 19, for נִכּוֹל 'we are able'), תֵּיכְלוּן (Josh. 24. 19, for תִּכְלוּן 'you are able'). For OJ forms having shewa as their preformative vowel see note 2.

Stem vowels. 2. Imperff. Peal with $\bar{e}$ as their stem vowel are יִתֵּיב (OTA יֵיתַב) and יֵיהִיב (PTM occasionally). In OJ imperf. forms like יְלִיד (Gen. 3. 16) and יְזִיף (Deut. 15. 6) are found occasionally.

Imperat. 3*. The imperatt. Peal are treated like the imperatt. of verbs initial nun. In PTM the initial radical is sometimes preserved (יְהַבוּן, יְהַב).

Aphel. 4*. The preformative vowel of the Aphel is generally $\bar{o}$ (אוֹנֵיק, אוֹטֵיב). Where $\bar{e}$ occurs in the MSS. it is frequently due to textual error (Dalman, p. 307 f.). Dalman recognizes אֵילֵיל in OJ and אֵיתֵיב and אֵיתַר as possibly correct in PTM הֵיבֵל occurs in OTA (Ezra 5. 14, 7. 15).

5*. In OJ הוֹדַע is used for אוֹדַע and the uncontracted forms יְהוֹדַע

and מְהוֹדַע more often, probably, than the contracted forms. Cf. § 16, note 4.

Shaphel.   **6.** The Shaphel שֵׁיזֵיב (OTA שֵׁיזֵב) ' rescue ' has no P^eal in use (? = שֵׁעֲזֵיב). סוֹבֵל (Ezra 6. 3) may be regarded as a causative of יבל, with ס as in some Syriac forms.   For שֵׁיצִי (? from יצא) see § 27, note 8.

Ithp^eel.   **7.** For elision of yodh in Ithp^eel forms see § 25, note 7.

יְהַב   **8.** In PTM forms with elided ה are used (e.g. יַבִית = יְהַבִית, *Chrest.* 29. 8). In OJ and OTA the imperf. and infin. of נתן take the place of the corresponding parts of יהב and are the only parts of נתן in use (see § 24, note 8). In PTM they are alternatives to יֵיהַב or יֵיהֵיב and מֵיהַב.

OTA.   **9.** For a synopsis of the forms of OTA see table, p. 96. In P^eal perff. and imperff. the stem vowel *i* corresponds to OJ *e* (יְתִב; יְכֵל, יְתֵב). In the imperf. P^eal preformative *ĭ* and *ē* both occur (יֵיסַב, יִבֵּל). יְדַע is always, erroneously, dissimilated to יִנְדַע (seven times). The normal Haphel form is like הוֹתֵב (cf. note 4) and a Hophal form (הוּסַף) occurs once. See also notes 6 and 8.

§ 27. VERBS FINAL YODH AND ALEPH

ITTAPHAL.	ITHPAAL.	ITP^HE^EL.	APH_EL.	PAEL.	P^EAL.	
אִתַּחֲזִי	אִתְחֲזִי	אִתְחֲזִי	אַחְזִי	חַזִּי	חֲזָא	perf.
אִתַּחֲזָא	אִתְחֲזָא	אִתְחֲזָא				
יִתַּחֲזִי	יִתְחֲזִי	יִתְחֲזֵי	יַחְזֵי	יְחַזִּי	יֶחְזֵי	imperf.
	יִתְחֲזָא					
אִתַּחֲזִי	אִתְחֲזִי	אִתְחֲזִי	אַחְזִי	חַזִּי	חֲזִי	imperat.
אִתַּחֲזָאָה	אִתְחֲזָאָה	אִתְחֲזָאָה	אַחְזָאָה	חַזָּאָה	מֶחְזֵי	infin.
מִתַּחֲזְיָא	מִתְחֲזְיָא	מִתְחֲזְיָא	מַחְזְיָא	מְחַזְיָא		PTM
(מִתַּחֲזֵי	מִתְחֲזֵי	מִתְחֲזֵי	מַחְזֵי	מְחַזֵּי	חָזֵי	act. ptc.
מִתַּחֲזָא)				מְחַזָּא	חֲזֵי	pass. ptc.
				מְחַזִּי		PTM

Final vowels of stem.   **1*.** In the bare stem forms, without an inflexional ending, the final radical coalesces with the preceding vowel into *ī* or *ē* or *ă* or *ā*. *ā* occurs only in the perfect Pᵉal (3 s. m.) and in the OJ adverbial infin. (note 6). *ă* comes from *ai* (cf. § 13, note 2) and the forms of the paradigm in which it is found seem to be peculiar to OJ (see, however, note 6).   In OJ and PTM the distinctive orthography הֲוָה is more common, in this verb, than הֲוָא (cf. הוא).

2*. Intransitive perfects Pᵉal ending in *ī* in OJ are: סְנִי, שְׁתִי, צְבִי, חֲדִי, &c. שְׁתִי (or אִשְׁתִּי, with prosthetic vowel) is the only form of the kind in PTM (Dalman). In OTA שתי (or אִשְׁתִּי) and צבי occur.

3. .Where *ī* appears in the final syllable of imperfects, it may be regarded as due to scribal error (Dalman).

4*. In Yemenite MSS. Pᵉal imperatt. of the form חֲוִי are corrections of חֲוַי under the influence of Hebrew (Diettrich, *ZATW.*, xx, p. 151).

Infin. forms.   **5*.** In OJ the third radical of feminine infinn. is written aleph but pronounced yodh (cf. § 23, note 9).   The writing of yodh twice in forms like מְחַזְיָיא, &c., is a characteristic of unvocalized MSS. ה is used in PTM less frequently than א to denote the feminine ending of infinitives.

6. In OJ an infin. Pᵉal of the form מִחְזָא is used as an adverbial infin. (cf. § 20, note 7). The PTM form מחזא may have been pronounced מְחֲזָא, from מִחְזַי. In 25. ii. 4 Dalman points *ā* in the final syllable (לְמִחְזָא).

Pass. partic.   **7*.** The passive partic. Pᵉal is sometimes pointed with final *ī* by supralinear MSS. (Deut. 25. 10, Josh. 7. 10).

Shaphel.   **8.** The Shaphel form שֵׁיצֵי 'complete', may be derived from יְצָא. For the *ē* of the preformative syllable see § 26, notes 4 and 6.

OTA.   **9.** The vocalic endings of the uninflected forms of the perff., imperff., and participles of OTA are *ā*, *ī*, and *ē*, as in

OJ (see table, p. 96). Final yodh is written when the vowel is *ī*
(הִתְנַבִּי) and in יִתְקְרֵי (Dan. 5. 12). In other cases—when the final
vowel is *ā* or *ē*—א or ה is written at the end of the word, without
any precise distinction between them. Examples: בְּעָא and בְּעָה;
בְּנָה. For the form בְּעָא and בְּעָה; מִבְעָא; יִבְעֵא. For the form אֱוֶה (Dan. 3. 22)
see § 25, note 9. In Ezra 6. 15 the Kethibh is שֵׁיצִיא, the Qᵉre שֵׁיצִי
or שֵׁצִי.

10. There are three examples of a 2 s. m. imperat. in OTA, one
Pael (מֶנִּי, Ezra 7. 25, for מַנִּי) and two Pᵉals (חֱיִי, in Dan. 2. 4, &c.,
and שָׂא, Ezra 5. 15, from נְשָׂא).

11. The third radical of the infinitives of the derived stems is
always yodh in the Kᵉthibh of MT (הַשְׁנָיָה, &c). There are, however,
supralinear and other MSS. in which aleph is read, as in OJ, by the
Qᵉre (see Strack's notes on Daniel 2. 10 and 6. 9).

12. The forms קֱרִי (Ezra 4. 18, 23) and גְּלִי (Dan. 2. 30) or גְּלִי
(Dan. 2. 19) and the plural רְמִיו (Dan. 3. 21, 7. 9) are examples of
perfect Pᵉīls (§ 16, note 11).

§ 28. VERBS FINAL YODH AND ALEPH
(perfect tenses)

APHEL.		PEAL.		PEAL.		
PTM	OJ	PTM	OJ	PTM	OJ	
	אַחְוִי		שְׁתִי		חֲזָא	3 s. m.
אחזיית	אַחְוִיאַת	שתיית	שְׁתִיאַת		חֲזָת	f.
אַחְוִיתָא -ת		שְׁתִיתָא -ת		חֲוֵיתָא -ת		2 s. m.
	אַחְוִית		שְׁתִית		חֲוֵית	f.
אַחְוִיתִי -ת		שְׁתִיתִי -ת		חֲוֵיתִי -ת		1 s. com.
אַחְוֹן	אַחְוִיאוּ	שְׁתוֹן	שְׁתִיאוּ	חֲזוֹן	חֲזוֹ	3 pl. m.
אַחְוָן	אַחְוִיאָה	—	שְׁתִיאָה	חֲזָן	חֲזָאָה	f.
	אַחְוִיתוּן		שְׁתִיתוּן		חֲוֵיתוֹן	2 pl. m.
	אַחְוִיתִין		שְׁתִיתִין		חֲוֵיתִין	f.
אַחְוִינַן	אַחְוִינָא	שְׁתִינַן	שְׁתִינָא	חֲוֵינַן	חֲוֵינָא	1 pl. com.

Endings.   1*. The OJ plural terminations וֹ (3 masc.) and
תוֹן (2 masc.) are peculiar to this class of verbs and are used in the
Peal only.   Dalman makes the corresponding endings of PTM *ōn*
and *tūn* (?) and extends the use of *ōn* to all perfects, in accordance
with the analogy of OJ imperfects.

2*. The distinctive endings תָא and תִי occur frequently in OJ and
to a less extent in PTM.   In OTA the endings of the 2 sing. masc.
and 1 sing. are תָ and ת respectively, and there is no example of
2 s. f.

3rd radical.   3*. Before all consonantal endings the third
radical of these verbs coalesces with the preceding stem vowel into
ē or *ī*, as shown in the table.   In *ī* perfects the reading *ē*, for *ī*, by
Yemenite MSS. is due to late correctors (Diettrich, *ZATW.*, vol. xx,
p. 151 f.).

4*. In the 3 s. f. of *ī* perfects and in the 3 pl. f. of all perfects,
OJ retains consonantal aleph (pronounced as yodh) and PTM
consonantal yodh (וַנַּיַת, 18. 3 ; שָׁרִיַת, 21. ii. 7).   There are two
cases in OTA, both of which agree with PTM in writing yodh
(אֶתְכְּרִיַת, Dan. 7. 15, and הֵיתָיִת, Dan. 6. 18).   In MT these two
forms follow two different systems of punctuation.   One of the
MSS. used by Strack supplies the variant reading הֵיתָיִת.   In PTM
אחזיית and אחזיין are unvocalized forms for אֲחֲזִיַת (? אֲחֲזַיִת or אֲחֲזַת)
and אֲחֲזַיִן.   In OJ א appears also in the 3 pl. m. of all *ī* perfects.

5. In PTM forms of the 3 s. f. and 3 pl. m. perf. Peal, with consonantal yodh retained, sometimes occur.   Presumably they were
pronounced like חֲוִיַת and חֲוִיִּן respectively (§ 17).   Dalman's
pointing of חֲמִיַת (22. 19) and בְּעִיַת (27. 2) seems to follow the
analogy of the OTA (Hophal) form הֵיתָיִת (note 4).   In OTA the
Kethibh preserves one 3 s. f. perf. Peal with consonantal yodh
(מטית, Dan. 4. 21).

OTA.   6. In OTA before consonantal terminations the final
syllable of the stem becomes *ī* in *ī* perfects (מַנִּיִת), *ai* in the 2 s. m.

of ordinary perff. Peal (חֲוֵיתָ) and in בְּנַיְתַהּ or בְּנֵיתַהּ 'I have built it' (Dan. 4. 27), ē in other forms (בְּעֵינָא, חֲוֵית). See also note 2.

7. In the 3 sing. fem. perf. Peal the forms חֲוָת and חֲוָת are written by MT without discrimination. Strack uniformly prints חֲוָת. In other respects the 3 s. f. of perfect tenses agrees with PTM (see notes 4 and 5). There is no example in OTA of a pl. fem. perf.

8. In one 3 pl. m. form (הֵיתָיוּ, § 31, note 6) consonantal yodh is retained and the vocalization is that of the normal verb (§ 17). With this exception the 3 pl. m. is like that of OJ (בְּעוֹ), with a variation of orthography in the ī perfects (שַׁוִּיוּ, אֶשְׁתִּיוּ), which is also found in some MSS. of OJ (Berliner, *Massorah*, p. 92). In Dan. 6. 17 and 6. 25 Strack's supralinear text reads הַיְתָיוּ. The only case of a 2 pl. m. is חֲוֵיתוּן (Dan. 2. 8), for which supralinear MSS. read חֲוֵיתוֹן.

9. Baer's reading of seghol for ṣere in the final syllable of pausal imperff. Pael and Haphel (Dan. 2. 4, 7, 24 and 5. 12) is not accepted by Strack.

§ 29. VERBS FINAL YODH AND ALEPH
(imperfects, imperatives and infinitives)

Peal.

PLURAL.	SINGULAR. PTM	OJ	IMPERFECT.
יֶחֱזוֹן		יֶחֱזֵי	3 masc.
יֶחֶזְיָן		תֶּחֱזֵי	fem.
תֶּחֶזוֹן		תֶּחֱזֵי	2 masc.
תֶּחֶזְיָן	תחזיין	תֶּחֱזַן	fem.
	תחזיי		
נֶחֱזֵי		אֶחֱזֵי	1 com.

PTM Aphel.	OJ		PTM PeAL.	OJ	Imperative.
	אַחְוִי			חֲוִי	2 s. m.
אַחְוִי	אַחְוָא		חֲוִי	חֲוָא	f.
אַחְווֹן	אַחְווֹ		חֲזוֹן	חֲזוֹ	2 pl. m.
—	—		—	חֲוָאָה	f.

Imperff. **1*.** The imperfect plur 1 masc. termination _ōn_ is known from the MSS. of OJ and OTA and is extended by analogy to PTM. The 2. s. f. endings in PTM are read by Dalman (p. 339) as _ain_ and _ai_ respectively. תחויין might be understood to signify תִּחְוְיָן (§ 2. 1).

2*. Consonantal yodh is retained by OJ and PTM in the 2 and 3 plur. fem. of all imperfects (cf. OTA לְהַחֲוָיָה, Dan. 5. 17). For the 2 s. f. in PTM see note 1.

3. Forms like אֲחֲוֵי (given in Dalman's paradigm) sometimes occur for אַחְוֵי (Gen. 24. 14, Merx), but are characteristic of the later Yemenite MSS. (§ 18, note 3).

Imperat. **4*.** The PTM imperative ending _ōn_ is got by analogy from the _ō_ of OJ and OTA. The 2 s. f. ending _ai_ is shortened from _ain_ and is the only ending of which Dalman gives examples from PTM. In OJ _ă_ = _ai_ (cf. § 27, note 1). The 2 plur. fem. form occurs in 2 Sam. 1. 24 (בכאה).

5. Shortened imperatives (2 s. m.) are found in OJ. Examples: אֶשְׁתְּ (Peal—Gen. 24. 14), שַׁו (Pael—Gen. 24. 2), אַעֵד or אַעַד (Aphel—Exod. 33. 5).

6*. The 2 s. m. imperat. of the derived stems is the same as the 3 s. m. perf. in OJ and PTM, the 2 pl. m. of all stems is the same as 3 pl. m. perf. in PTM and the Peal imperat. 2 plur. is the same as the 3 plur. perf. in OJ. Cf. § 19, note 4.

Infinn. **7.** Infinitives of the form מִשְׁתַּיָא are found in PTM. Cf. Ezra 5. 9, מִבְנְיָה.

8. Peal infinitives with suffixes are treated in OJ like plural

nouns (§ 13, note 7), except that אֲ is used for *ai* as the suffix of
the 1st singular and that הֲ is employed for הָאֲ. Examples:
מַחְזוֹהִי, מֶחֱזָא. PTM has forms like מְחַמְיֵנֵּהּ or מְחַמְיֵנֵּהּ (see § 37,
note 6). In OTA, stems with consonantal yodh are used (מְצַבְּיֵהּ,
Dan. 4. 32).

9. Infinitives of the derived stems with suffixes retain the third
radical in OJ (אַשְׁקָיוּתֵיהּ, Gen. 24. 9) and are treated like feminine
nouns of the F class (§ 12, note 9) in PTM (e. g. מְמַנָּיְתֵיהּ from the
Pael infinitive מְמַנָּיָא).

OTA. 10. The inflexions of imperfects and imperatt. in OTA,
so far as examples are found, are the same as in OJ (cf. notes 1, 2,
and 4). There is no case of a feminine imperat. nor of a 2 s. f.
imperf. The form יִשְׁתַּנּוֹ (Dan. 5. 10), with *ō* for *ōn*, may be a
special jussive form (Strack). Cf. § 38, note 3. For the infinitives see notes 7 and 8.

§ 30. VERBS FINAL YODH AND ALEPH
(inflexion of participles)

PAEL.	PEAL.	PEAL.	
Active ptc.	*Pass. ptc.*	*Act. ptc.*	
מְכַסֵּי	חֲזֵי	חָזֵי	Sing. m.
מְכַסְּיָא	חַזְיָא	חָזְיָא	f.
מְכַסַּן, מְכַסַּיִן	חֲזַן, חֲזַיִן	חָזַן, חָזַיִן	Plur. m.
מְכַסְּיָן	חַזְיָן	חָזְיָן	f.

1*. In the feminine singular and plural of participles consonantal
yodh is always retained and in the masc. plural the ending is *ain*
in OTA and usually in PTM. In OJ the masc. plural ending is
always *ăn*, and this form also occurs in PTM.

2*. Participles used as nouns employ the plural termination
ewān (§ 8, note 11). Examples: רָעֲוָן, from רָעֵי 'shepherd', and
אָסְוָן, from אָסֵי 'physician'.

3*. In the inflected forms, when the middle radical is a guttural or a doubled consonant, the supralinear MSS. regularly indicate vocal shewa before consonantal yodh (רַעְיָא‎, מְחַפְּיָן‎). Except in these cases vocal shewa is seldom represented (Dalman, p. 340), but should be pronounced in reading in accordance with the general analogy of participle forms, except in the singular fem. of the Peal passive partic. (cf. § 10, note 14).

4*. Words like חֲזִי‎ with pronominal suffixes attached are inflected in three ways: (1) the suffixes may unite with the termination *ē* as with a plural ending (מָחוֹהִי‎, Deut. 25. 11), or (2) the final radical yodh may be retained ((בְּרָיִךְ‎, 25. ii. 8, from בְּרִי‎), or (3) instead of yodh, aleph may be used. In OJ סָנֵי‎ always retains א‎ with suffixes (Gen. 14. 20, Exod. 20. 5, Deut. 5. 9, 7. 15, 30. 7, 2 Sam. 19. 7, 22. 18, Jer. 49. 7). So also שָׂנְאָךְ‎, Dan. 4. 16, which is the only example of a suffixed form of these participles in OTA.

5. Examples of tense forms like those of § 21, note 7, are חֲוֵינָא‎ (26. 6), fem. שָׁרְיָנָא‎ (Dalman, p. 352), מַשְׁקֵית‎ (Deut. 11. 10—Kahle, p. 16), בָּעֵינַן‎ (29. 25). The 1 sing. masc. of this tense is always wrongly pointed like חֲוֵינָא‎ in the Yemenite MSS.

§ 31.[1]   הֲלַךְ‎, חֲיָא‎, הֲוָה‎, אֲתָא‎

APHEL.	PeAL.	PeAL.	APHEL.	PeAL.	
אַחִי‎	חֲיָא‎	הֲוָה‎	אִיתִי, אֵיתִי‎	אֲתָא‎	perf.
			אַתִיאוּ, אֵיתִיאוּ‎	אֲתוֹ‎	
יַחֵי‎	יֵיחֵי‎	יְהֵוֵי, יְהֵי‎	יַיתֵי‎	יֵיתֵי‎	imperf.
		יְהֵווֹן, יְהוֹן‎	יַיתוֹן‎	יֵיתוֹן‎	
	חֲיִי‎	הֲוִי‎	אִיתָא‎	אִיתָא‎	imperat.
			אִיתוֹ‎	אִיתוֹ‎	
אַחָיָה‎		מֶהֱוֵי‎	אִיתָאָה‎	מֵיתֵי‎	infin.
			מֵיתָיָא‎		PTM
מַחֵי‎	חָיֵי‎	הֲוֵי‎	מֵיתֵי‎	אָתֵי‎	partic.

[1] To be passed over on a first reading of the grammar.

1. Several verbs, having stems with both initial aleph and final aleph or yodh, are treated like אֲתָא (אבא, אוֹא, אסא, אפא). Of these only אֲתָא has a shortened imperat. form (§ 25, note 4).

2. The imperff. and imperatt. Peal and Aphel of אתא are written alike, but are distinguished in pronunciation (see note 3). מֵיתֵי is both infin. Peal and partic. Aphel.

Imperat. 3. In the imperat. Peal the OJ supralinear form אִיתָא is equivalent to אֲתָא (§ 25, note 3) and the final vowel represents an original *ai*. In PTM אֱתִי (24. ii. 13), אֲתָא (איתָא, 22. ii. 8), and תָא (§ 25, note 4) are all used. In Berliner's *Onkelos ī* is written in אִיתָא, אִיתוֹ, &c. (cf. אֱיֵיל). The final vowel of אִיתָא may be corrected into ă (similarly in the case of אֲיְתָא, 22. ii. 8).

4. The 2 s. f. imperat. Peal of אתא is אִיתָא (1 Kings 1. 12— Kahle, p. 29) or אֱתִי (*Chrest.* 29. 22). Cf. § 29, note 4. An alternative Aphel imper. 2 plur. masc. אִיתִיאוּ (Gen. 42. 34) is given by Dalman (p. 356).

5. μαραναθά (1 Cor. 16. 22) is explained by Dalman (p. 152, note 3) as being מָרָנָא תָא ' Come, our Lord'. WH and von Soden both divide the word into μαρὰν ἀθά.

OTA. 6. For אֲתָא see table at the end of this section. The OTA passive forms הֵיתָיַת (Dan. 6. 18) and הֵיתָיִו (Dan. 3. 13) are explained as Hophal forms = הוּתָיַת (3 s. f. perf.) and הוּתָיִו (3 pl. m. perf.) respectively (Strack).

הוה. **7.** In OJ the longer forms of the imperf. Peal of הֲוָה are used only in the plural and (as alternatives) along with אֵיהֵי or אֱהֵי in the 1 sing. In PTM short and long forms are used indifferently and both יְהֵא and יֵּ occur. For PTM לִהְוֵי and OTA לֶהֱוֵא, &c., see § 18, note 6. The 3 sing. fem. impf. in OTA is תֶּהֱוֵא or תְּהֵוֵה. No shortened forms occur in OTA.

8. In the MSS. published by Kahle the shortened forms of the Peal imperf. of הֲוָה are written יְהֵי and יְהוֹן, with the original preformative vowel retained (cf. § 2. 9).

חיא.   **9.** In the verb חֲיָא the medial radical yodh is generally suppressed in OJ and PTM in the imperfect (and infin.) Peal and in all parts of the Aphel. The same forms are used in Syriac. Cf. also יְהֵי and Hebrew יְחִי. For OTA see table below.

הלך.   **10.** In OJ and OTA the impf. and infin. of הלך elide the medial *l* and assume the forms יְהָךְ (plur. יְהָכוּן) and מְהָךְ respectively (cf. סליק, § 24, note 7). In the perfect and participle OJ uses only Pael forms (cf. OTA מְהַלֵּךְ). The imperf. and infin. Pael also sometimes occur in OJ.

HAPHEL.	PᵉAL.	PᵉAL.	HAPHEL.	PᵉAL.	OTA
		הֲוָא, הֲוָה	הַיְתִי	אֲתָה, אֲתָא	perf.
		הֲוֹ	הַיְתִיו	אֲתוֹ	
		לֶהֱוֵא			imperf.
		לֶהֱוֹן			
	חֲיִי	הֲוִי		אֱתוֹ	imperat.
			הַיְתָיָה (הֵיתָיָה)	מֵתָא	infin.
מֶחָא				אָתֵה	partic.

§ 32. MONOSYLLABIC STEMS (ע"י)

ITTAPHAL.	ITHPᵉEL.	APHEL.	PᵉAL.	
	PTM	OJ AND PTM		
אִתְּקַם	אִתְּקִים	אִתְקַם	אֲקִים	קָם	perf.
אִתּוֹקַם					PTM
יִתְּקַם	יִתְּקִים	יִתְקַם	יְקִים	יְקוּם	imperf.
—	אִתְּקִים	אִתְקַם	אֲקִים	קוּם	imperat.
—	—	אִתְקָמָא	אֲקָמָא	מְקָם	infin.
		מִתְּקָמָא	מְקָמָא	מְקוֹם	PTM
מִתְּקַם	מִתְּקִים	מִתְקַם	מְקִים	קָאִים	partic. act.
				קִים	partic. pass.

Stem vowels. **1.** The stem vowels of the Peal forms some-times differ from those of the table. **Perfects in ī** are מִית ' die ', סִיב ' be old ', and רִיר ' spit '. **Imperfects in ē** are יְבֵית, יְקֵים, and יְדֵין (or יְדוּן) from בָּת ' pass the night ', סָם ' place ', and דָּן ' judge '. **Verbs final guttural** generally have ŭ in the imperf. and imperat. (e.g. יְנוּחַ), but זָע ' shake ' has imperf. יְזוּעַ and imperat. זַע (plur. זוּעוּ). Pathaḥ furtive no doubt always followed ŭ in speech, whether written or not (§ 2. 5). Verbs with imperff. in ē have **imperatives in ī** (בִּית, Judg. 19. 6 and 9).

2*. In supralinear MSS. the Aphel stem vowel ē (perf. and imperat.) is sometimes written ī and the stem vowel ī (imperf. and partic.) is sometimes written ē. The stem vowel of the 3 s. m. perf. Aphel with pronominal suffixes appears to be normally ī (אֲקִימַהּ, Josh. 24. 26 ; Gen. 47. 7, Num. 27. 22 ; Dan. 3. 1, 5. 11).

Preformative vowels. **3.** The preformative vowels of the Peal are sometimes treated according to the analogy of verbs ע״ע (§ 34), so that forms like יְקוּם and יֵיחוּם, מְקָם and מֵיחוּם occur. Examples : יְמוּת, Num. 35. 25 (Kahle, p. 9), יְתוּב, Jer. 18. 8 (Kahle, p. 38), יֵיחוּם, Exod. 12. 23.

4*. The preformative vowel of the imperff., imperatt., infinn., and particc. Aphel is often written ā in supralinear MSS. Examples : אָתְבָא אָתִיב (Gen. 24. 5—Merx), אָנְחָא (Judg. 1. 1), אָנַח (2 Sam. 24. 16—Kahle, p. 27), אָקֵים (2 Sam. 24. 18—Kahle, p. 27), מָנַח (Exod. 17. 11—Dalman, p. 324). In OTA preformative ā occurs in an imperfect (Dan. 2. 44) and a partic. (Dan. 5. 19) and in the uncontracted forms יְהָקִים (Dan. 5. 21, 6. 16) and מְהָקִים (Dan. 2. 21). In PTM the corresponding vowel is ō.

5*. When supralinear pathaḥ is written in the perfect and imperative Aphel instead of preformative vocal shewa, it may be understood to denote vocal shewa (§ 2. 7), rather than to indicate a form according to the analogy of verbs ע״ע (§ 34).

Ithpeel. **6.** In OJ the stem vowel of the Ithpeel is sometimes

written ă (אִתְּנַח, Judg. 5. 20) and the נ of the preformative syllable
may become ד before initial ד (hence אִתְּדָן = אִתְּדָּן).

Intensives. 7*. The intensive forms in use are קָיֵם, קַיַּם (OJ
supralinear), קוֹמֵם, קָמֵם (OJ supralinear), and קַמְקֵם. The passive
of the Palpel is like מְטַלְטַל (Gen. 4. 12) or מְטֻלְטָל (Gen. 4. 16).

Verbs medial waw. 8*. Verbs having consonantal waw as
their medial radical are רְוַח, רָוַח, חֲוַר, צְוַח, עֲוַר 'rejoice', &c., also
some verbs having both medial waw and final yodh, שְׁוָא, הֲוָה, &c.

OTA. 9. In OTA both the stem vowels and the preformative
vowels of the PᵉAL and HAPHEL are normally those of the table
above. In the 3 s. m. pf. Haphel the stem vowel ī occurs as an
alternative to ē (Dan. 2. 14, 6. 2) and in the participle (Dan. 2. 21)
and the imperf. sing. (Dan. 2. 44, 5. 21, 6. 16) ē occurs as an alternative to ī. Preformative ḥateph seghol occurs in one Haphel
form in most (?) MSS. (הֲקִימָה, Dan. 5. 11). The stem vowel of the
HITHPᵉEL is ā in one verb (יִתְּשָׂם) and ī in another (יִתְּוֵן). The
only INTENSIVE FORMS are קַיָּמָה (Dan. 6. 8), מְרוֹמֵם (Dan.
4. 34) and הִתְרוֹמַמְתָּ (Dan. 5. 23). There is one HOPHAL, הֻקִימַת
(Dan. 7. 4, 5). The peculiar passive form שְׁמַת (Dan. 6. 18) should
perhaps be written שֻׁמַת (cf. § 16, note 11). See also notes 2
and 4.

§ 33. MONOSYLLABIC STEMS (inflected forms)

APHEL.		PᵉAL.		
Imperat.	*Perfect.*	*Partic.*	*Perfect.*	
אָקֵים	אָקֵים	קָאֵים, קָיֵם	מִית	קָם
אָקִימִי	אָקֵימַת	קָיְמָא	מִיתַת	קַמַת
אָקֵימְתְּ -תָּא	אֲקֵימְתְּ -תָּא		מֵיתְתְּ -תָּא	קַמְתְּ -תָּא
. . .			. . .	. . .
אֲקִימוּ	אֲקִימוּ	קָיְמִין	מִיתוּ	קָמוּ
אֲקִימָא	אֲקִימָא	קָיְמָן	(מִיתָא ?)	קָמָא

Pᵉal perff. **1*.** The forms of the table are those of the supra-linear punctuation. The stem vowel of the perf. Pᵉal is *ā* only in the 3 s. m. and 3 pl. m. In Syriac and OTA *ā* is the stem vowel throughout the perf. Pᵉal, and this pointing is used by Dalman in his *Dialektproben*. The inflected forms of מִית are treated like those of perfects in ṣere.

Particc. **2*.** In OJ (and sometimes in PTM) the uninflected participle Pᵉal has the form of verbs medial aleph. In the inflected forms yodh is written for aleph in both OJ and PTM. In OTA the inflected forms have א in the Kᵉthibh and י in the Qᵉre, except in קָאֲמַיָּא (Dan. 7. 16). The inflected participle forms of verbs medial aleph retain א in OJ and sometimes in PTM (1 Sam. 8. 10, 1 Kings 2. 20; *Chrest.*, 20. 14). Cf. § 23, note 9, and Dalman, p. 305.

OTA. **3.** In OTA the termination of the 1 s. pf. is *ĕth* (שָׂמֵת, Ezra 6. 12; הֲקִימֵת, Dan. 3. 14). For the form יַחִיטוּ (Ezra 4. 12) see § 35, note 5.

§ 34. PARTIALLY MONOSYLLABIC STEMS (ע"ע)

APHEL.		PeAL.		
אַעֵיל	אַבֵּין	עַל	בַּז (בָּז)	perf.
יַעֵיל	יַבֵּין	יֵיעוֹל	יְבוֹז	imperf.
אַעֵיל	אַבֵּין	עוֹל	בּוֹז	imperat.
אַעָלָא	אַבְזָא	מֵיעַל	מִבַּז	infin.
מַעֵיל	מַבֵּין	עָלֵיל	בָּזֵין	partic. act.
מַעַל	מַבַּז	עָלֵיל	בְּזֵין	ptc. pass.

Disyllabic stems. **1*.** Disyllabic stems are used in the Pᵉal participles, all intensive forms, Ithpᵉels, and Shaphels. Examples: שַׁכְלִיל, אִתְבְּזִיז, מַלֵּיל. See also § 35, note 4.

2*. The intensive forms are of the types עַלֵּיל, עוֹלֵיל (especially PTM), עָלֵיל (OJ), and עַלְעֵיל. עַיֵּיל is borrowed from the ע״י stems (§ 32). The use of עָלֵיל is a special feature of the supralinear vocalization. מְקַצַץ (25. 4) is the passive participle of this form.

Stem vowels.   3*. The stem vowel of the 3 s. m. perf. Pᵉal, which is pathaḥ in Syriac and OTA, is always *ā* in the supralinear vocalization of OJ, following the analogy of the verbs of § 32. The stem vowel of the imperf. Pᵉal is either *ō* or *ă* (יַחַם, יִבּוֹז).

Preform. vowels.   4*. The imperf., imperat., and infin. Pᵉal and all the tenses of the Aphel have the same forms as the corresponding parts of verbs initial nun (§ 24). In the imperf. and infin. Pᵉal preformative *ĭ* is lengthened to *ē* before an initial stem guttural, but is retained before initial resh (יָרֹק, Lev. 15. 8). This treatment is reversed in the only two cases that occur in OTA (מְחַן, Dan. 4. 24; תֵּרַע, Dan. 2. 40).

Participles.   5. In PTM the participle form עַיֵּיל (§ 32) is sometimes used in place of עָלֵיל. In OJ contracted plurals like עָלִין, for עָלְלִין, are a feature of supralinear texts. In OTA עללין (Kᵉthibh) is replaced by עָלִין or עָלִּין or עַלִּין (Dan. 4. 4, 5. 8).

6. Aphel participles like מיקל and מיצן in PTM are viewed as Hebraisms by Dalman.

7. מַעֲלָה (25. 5), from מַעַל, follows the ordinary rule for the inflexion of participles. For מַקֵּילִין (23. 8) see § 21, note 6.

Borrowed forms.   8*. The forms appropriate to עו״י stems (§ 32) are transferred to verbs of this class in the cases named in notes 2, 3, and 5, and in others also (e.g. in Judg. 6. 26 תְּקוּץ = תְּקוּץ).

Ittaphal.   9. The Ittaphal forms are like אִתָּעַל and אִתָּחַל.

OTA.   10. For the Pᵉal perf. see note 3, and for the only examples of imperf. infin. and partic. see notes 4 and 5. There are three types of INTENSIVES in OTA: מַלֵּל (three verbs), מְרָעַע (Dan. 2. 40), and אֶשְׁתּוֹמַם (Dan. 4. 16). In the HAPHEL, preformative pathaḥ becomes seghol before עָ (הֶעָלָה, Dan. 5. 7). There are two cases of erroneously dissimilated Haphel forms (הַנְעֵל, Dan. 2. 25, 6. 19, and הַנְעָלָה, Dan. 4. 3). Cf. § 26, note 9. For normal Haphel forms see table p. 96. A HOPHAL form of one verb is found (הֻעַל).

§ 35. PARTIALLY MONOSYLLABIC STEMS
(inflected forms)

APHEL.		PEAL.	
PERFECT.		**PERFECT.**	
Plur.	Sing.	Plur.	Sing.	
אַעֵילוּ	אַעֵיל	עַלּוּ (עָלוּ)	עַל (עָל)	3 masc.
אַעֵילָא	אַעֵילַת	עַלָּא	עַלַּת	fem.
אַעֵילְתּוּן	אַעֵילְתְּ -תָּא	עַלְתּוּן	עַלְתְּ -תָּא	2 masc.
אַעֵילְתִּין	אַעֵילְתְּ	עַלְתִּין	עַלְתְּ	fem.
אַעֵילְנָא	אַעֵילִית	עַלְנָא	עַלִּית	1 com.
IMPERFECT.		**IMPERFECT.**	
Plur.	Sing.	Plur.	Sing.	
יַעֲלוּן	יַעֵיל	יֵיעֲלוּן	יֵיעוֹל	3 masc.
תַּעֲלוּן	תַּעֵיל	תֵּיעֲלוּן	תֵּיעוֹל	2 masc.
נַעֵיל	אַעֵיל	נֵיעוֹל	אֵיעוֹל	1 com.
IMPERATIVE.		**IMPERATIVE.**	
Plur.	Sing.	Plur.	Sing.	
אַעֵילוּ	אַעֵיל	עוּלּוּ	עוֹל	2 masc.
אַעֵילָא	אַעֵילִי	עוּלָּא	עוּלִּי	fem.

1*. Following Dalman's precedent, and in accordance with the analogy of OTA, the final radical has been doubled in the above table, before vocalic endings, in the Peal perfect and imperative, but not in the Aphel. In Berliner's *Onkelos* doubling is not indicated in any tense.

2*. In the 3·pl. m. perf. Peal the stem vowel *ā* (appropriate to
ע״יִ stems) is sometimes written in supralinear MSS. for *ă*. The
only example of a 3 plur. masc. perf. Peal in OTA is treated in this
way (דָּקוּ, Dan, 2. 35). See also § 34, note 3.

3. Supralinear pathaḥ in imperf. forms like יַעֲלֹן (Deut. 10. 11—
Kahle, p. 15) may be regarded as representing ḥateph pathaḥ
(§ 2. 7).

4. Peal and Aphel forms like רקקת (PTM), עללת (Dan. 5. 10,
Kᵉthibh), and תַּמְלַל (Dan. 4. 9), with repetition of the final radical,
occur in PTM and OTA.

OTA. **5.** The distinctive features of OTA are as follows: In
the inflected forms of the imperative PᵉAL the stem vowel is *ŏ*
(גֻּדּוּ, Dan. 4. 11, 20). In the perfect HOPHAL some MSS.
double the final radical before the plural ending (הֻעַלּוּ, Dan. 5. 15),
others do not. In HAPHEL forms, when the stem vowel (*ē*)
becomes vocal shewa, it is written ḥateph seghol in some MSS.
(מַדְּקָה, Dan. 7. 7, 19, תְּדֶקְנַּה, Dan. 7. 23—Baer, Ginsburg, Strack).
Perhaps יַחִיטוּ (Ezra 4. 12) was originally intended for יַחֵטוּ (cf. § 2.
8, 9). But the tense, termination (§ 18, note 7) and possibly stem
vowel (cf. § 34, note 8) are all abnormal. There is no other
example of the 3 plur. imperf. Haphel of an ע״ע verb in OTA.
See also notes above, and for הַדֶּקֶת or הַדֵּקֶת (Dan. 2. 34, 45), § 17,
note 6.

§ 36. VERBAL SUFFIXES

1*. For the various forms of the accusative suffixes see pp. 90–
91. In PTM the suffixes added to verbal stems ending in a consonant are those of § 4 and the suffixes added to stems ending in
a vowel are presumably those of § 12, note 2, although the only
possible vocalic stem is the 2 sing. fem. perf. (for the 2 s. m. and the
3 pl. see notes 3 and 5). In OJ the variations from the suffixes of
§§ 4 and 12 are in the 1 singular, נִי or נִ֑ for *ī*, and in the 3 plural,

where the independent pronoun אָנּוּ is substituted for הוֹן (וֹן). For the forms of the suffixes added to the 3 s. f. perf. see note 6. In OJ, in agreement with the Hebrew text, the suffix of the 2 plural is rarely found. It seems never to occur with a 3 sing. masc. perf. stem.

2*. In OJ אָנּוּ is joined in writing to the verbal stem with which it is associated, א being omitted when the stem ends in a consonant and the form being reduced to נוּ with the 3 s. f. perf and to נוּ in union with stems ending in a vowel (שְׁלַחְתְּנוּ, שְׁלַחְתּוּן, שְׁלַחוּנוּ). The forms of the verbal stems are not modified before אָנּוּ except in the 1 s. perf., in which כְּתִיבַת, בַּתִּיבָת and אַכְתִּיבַת are used for כְּתָבִית, &c.

3*. The difference between PTM and OJ in the endings of the 3 plur. perf. and 2 plur. imperat. involves a further difference in the suffixes attached to these forms. PTM uses the suffixes appropriate to the consonantal ending *ŭn*, while OJ uses those required by the vocalic ending *ŭ*. Examples: אַפְּקוּנֵיה (25. ii. 2), אַפְּקוּהִי (Gen. 19. 16).

Perfect 3 s. m. and 3 pl. m. **4.** For the stem forms of the 3 s. m. and 3 pl. m. perfects Peal and Aphel with suffixes see paradigm, p. 90. Pael perfects are treated like Aphels. In the suffixed forms of the perfects Pael and Aphel the final stem vowel generally becomes vocal shewa both in the 3 sing. and the 3 plural (אַפְּקוּהִי, Gen. 19. 16), although sometimes the orthography of PTM presumably indicates the retention of the full vowel (20. ii. 2, אַמַלִיכוּנִי, 21. 1, אַמַלִיכוּנֵיה).

OJ plural forms are sometimes found in PTM (26. 8, נְצָחוּךְ). Sometimes the vowel points in Dalman's *Dialektproben* are unnecessarily those of OJ, instead of being those of PTM. In 21. ii. 7 יְהַבִינָן should be יְהַבוּנָן, and in 28. 5 אַרְפּוֹנָן should be אַרְפּוֹנָן.

2 sing. and 1 sing. **5.** In OJ and PTM the forms of the 1 sing. perf. with suffixes are like כְּתָבִת, &c. The 2 sing. masc. and 1 sing. com. with suffixes of the 3 s. m. or 3 pl. (where

ambiguity arises) are distinguished in OJ by the use of the form
כְּתַבְתְּ for the 2 s. m. But ambiguous forms with suffixes of the
3 sing. fem. like אַשְׁכַּחְתַּהּ 'I have found her' (Gen. 38. 22) and
'thou hast found her' (Gen. 38. 23) are in use. שְׁבַקְתַּנִי (Gen.
31. 28) = σαβαχθανεί (Matt. 27. 46), having a suffix of the first
person, can only mean 'thou hast forsaken me'. In PTM the
2 s. m. is clearly distinguished from the 1 sing. com. by its employ-
ment of the termination *inn* (note 8) before suffixes (שְׁבַקְתִּנִי,
אַשְׁכַּחְתִּנַּהּ). The 2 sing. fem. perf. is distinguished by its retention
of the old termination *î* before suffixes (אַשְׁכַּחְתִּיהָא).

3 s. f. **6*.** The 3 sing. fem. perf. with suffixes is sometimes
written as if it were 1 sing. com. (מְלַכְתֵּיהּ 'she counselled him',
Judg. 1. 14). All the cases noted by Praetorius (Judg. 1. 14) are
forms in which the suffix is 3 s. m. The unambiguous forms are:
שְׁלַחְתַּהּ, שְׁלַחְתֵּיהּ, שְׁלַחְתָּךְ ; שְׁלַחְתְּנוּן, שְׁלַחְתְּכוֹן, שְׁלַחְתָּנָא, שְׁלַחְתְּנִי.

1 plur. and 2 plur. **7.** The suffixed stem of the 1 plur. perf.
in OJ is the same as the independent stem, but written without א
(שְׁלַחְנָהִי). Instead of שְׁלַחְנָא the form שְׁלַחְנַהּ is used. In PTM the
forms שְׁלַחְנָת, &c., are used with suffixes. Dalman explains ת as
derived from the accus. particle יָת (§ 4, note 4). The suffixed stems
of the 2 plur. masc. perf. are like שְׁלַחְתּוּ in OJ (suffixes as § 12) and
like שְׁלַחְתּוּן in PTM (suffixes as in § 4).

Imperf. stems. **8*.** The stems of imperfects with suffixes are
treated similarly in OJ and PTM. The syllable *inn* is added to
the stems of all imperfects (cf. Hebrew יַעֲבְדֶנּוּ), except in OJ before
the 3 plur. masc. suffix. The suffixes are the same as those added
to perfect stems. (See paradigm, p. 90 f.). The orthography יִרְדְּפֻנּוּן
for יִרְדְּפֻנּוּן and יַרְדִּפֻנּוּן for יַרְדְּיפֻנּוּן in Yemenite MSS. is a Hebraism
due to late correctors (Diettrich in *ZATW*. xx. 152).

Imperat. stems. **9.** In OJ singular imperative stems with
suffixes remain unchanged and the suffixes are those of § 12, except
in the cases of the 1 sing. and 3 plural. In PTM the Pael and

Aphel singular imperat. stems with suffixes are identical with the
corresponding perfect stems. The Pᵉal imperat. stem is distinguished from its perfect by the vowels *ĭ* or *ŭ* following the initial
radical. These vowels are sometimes indicated in the MSS. by
yodh and waw respectively.

The imperative plural stem in OJ is like כְּתֻבוּ and in PTM like
כְּתֻבוּן (see paradigm, p. 91). Pael and Aphel perfect and imperative plural forms are generally not distinguishable. The Aphel
imperat. in OJ occasionally retains its final stem vowel (e. g. אַפֵּיקוּהָא
'bring her out' = אַפֵּקוּהָא).

ע״י stems. **10*.** The forms of ע״י verbs undergo no change
when suffixes are attached (but see § 32, note 2).

Syntax. **11.** The use of an anticipative pronominal suffix
before a definite accusative governed by a verb, an idiom characteristic of Syriac, is found occasionally in OJ (Gen. 39. 15, שַׁבְקֵיה
לִלְבָשֵׁיה לְוָתִי 'he left his garment beside me') and PTM (22. ii. 4,
פַּקְּדֵיה לִשְׁלִיחָא 'he ordered the messenger'; 21. 7, 22. ii. 6).

12. The subject of a dependent clause introduced by דְּ is also
sometimes preceded by an anticipative pronoun (16. 6, אַשְׁכְּחֵיה
דַּהֲוָה מְזַבֵּן 'he found that he had been selling'). It is idiomatic to
put the subject of such a dependent clause into the principal
sentence as an object (16. ii. 11, חֲמָא לְהָהוּא דְּזָבֵין דְּקָאִים בָּתְרֵיה
'he saw that the buyer was standing behind him ').

13. Occasionally the object pronoun of the 3 plural is used
indefinitely for 'some people' (28. 4, חֲמָתוּן קָטְלִין 'he saw some
men killing' (mice); for the verbal stem חמת see § 37, note 1).

§ 37.¹ VERBAL SUFFIXES WITH ל״א STEMS

Perf. 3 s. m. **1.** In PTM the termination of 3 s. m. of all
perfects with suffixes is treated like the ending of a feminine noun

---

¹ To be passed over on a first reading of the grammar.

(cf. § 36, note 7). Examples: חֲמִיתֵיהּ and חֲמַיְתֵיהּ (or חֲמֵיתֵיהּ),
אִיתְחֵיהּ, כַּסִּיתֵיהּ. In the derived stems these forms, when unvocalized, are the same as the 3 s. f. (note 4), and in the Peᵃl חֲמָתֵיהּ
is always ambiguous, 'he saw him' or 'she saw him' (note 5).

2. In OJ the 3 s. m. perf. Peᵃl with suffixes either retains (consonantal) א (חֲזָיֵהּ, חֲזָאָךְ, &c.) or is treated as ending in a vowel
(חֲזָהִי, חֲזָךְ). With אִנּוּן the suffixed forms are like חֲזָנּוּן.

3 s. m. and 3 pl. m. **3.** In OJ the 3 s. m. and 3 pl. m. perfects Pael and Aphel with suffixes generally preserve the third
radical yodh. Examples: אַשְׁרְיֵהּ (Gen. 2. 15), אַיְתְיַהּ (Gen. 2. 22),
אַטְעֲיַנִי (Gen. 3. 13), אֵיתִיוֹהִי (Judg. 1. 7). With אִנּוּן the ordinary
stem is used (אַחְזִינּוּן).

In PTM the third radical yodh is sometimes retained both in
Peᵃl perfects (25. iii. 7, מַחְיוּנֵיהּ = מַחְיוּגֵיהּ), and in perfects of the
derived stems (cf. notes 1 and 5).

3 s. f. **4.** In OJ and PTM the ending of the 3 s. f. of ī perfects
(§ 27) is generally contracted to ית. before suffixes. Examples:
אַשְׁקִיתֵיהּ, כַּפִּיתֵיהּ (Judg. 4. 19), אֵיתִיתָךְ (*Chrest.* 18. 13). In PTM
these are also imperative forms (note 7).

Perf. stems. **5.** In the other parts of the perfect tenses suffixes
are generally added to the unchanged verbal stem. Examples:
חֲזָתֵיהּ (3 s. f.), חֲזֵיתָהִי (OJ 2 s. m), חֲמַיְתֵיהּ (1 sing.), חֲזוֹהִי (OJ 3 pl.
perf. Peᵃl), חֲזוֹנֵיהּ (PTM 3 pl.). For חֲמֵינָתֵיהּ (1 plur.) see § 36,
note 7.

In some supralinear MSS. the ending of the 3 pl. m. pf. Peᵃl with
suffixes is written *ū* instead of *ō* (מְחוּהָא, Judg. 1. 8 ; מְחוּנּוּן, Judg.
1. 4).

Impf. stems. **6.** In all imperf. tenses the suffixed stem is made
by adding נ to the ordinary stem (§ 36, note 8). Examples:
יִחְזוֹנֵּיהּ, יַחְזֵיּנֵּיהּ. When אִנּוּן is used the forms are like that of יִחְזֵינּוּן.
In some supralinear MSS. the vowels before *nn* are *i* instead of *ē*,
and *ū* instead of *ō* (יִחְזוּנֵּיהּ, יַחְזֵיּנֵּיהּ). Cf. OTA, § 38, note 5.

Imperat. stems.   7. In OJ imperatives 2 s. m. and 2 pl. m. stems are unchanged when suffixes are added (אַחְוִינִי, חֲזֹוהִי).   In some MSS. *ū* is written for *ō* and forms with consonantal yodh are also found (אַחְוְיַנָא, Judg. 1. 24).

In PTM the termination *ī* of the 2 s. m. is treated like a feminine termination (23. ii. 7, אִיְתֵיתֵיה). 2 pl. m. forms are like אַרְפֹּונֻן (for which in 28. 5 Dalman puts אַרְפֹּנֻן).

Participles.   8. *nn* is used with other suffixed stems than those named above, e. g. with participles (29. 7, מְפַנִּינֵיה, i.e. מְפַנְּיִנֵּיה).

§ 38. VERBAL SUFFIXES IN OTA

Suffix forms.   1. The forms of the verbal suffixes in OTA and the treatment of the stems to which they are attached agree closely with the corresponding features of OJ.   The accusative pronoun 'them' is not expressed by a suffix but by some one of three independent pronouns—הִמֹּו (eight times), הִמֹּן (three times), and אִנּוּן (Dan. 6. 25).   The suffixes attached to verbal stems vary according as the stem ends in a consonant or a vowel.   In the former case, they are the same as the suffixes joined to nouns, except that נִי is ' me ' and that נָא is written for נָא_ in the only case of its occurrence (Dan. 2. 23).   In the latter case, the suffixes that actually occur are : נִי, ךְ (2 s. m.), הִי (§ 12), נָא, and כֹן.

Perf. stems.   2. The stems of the 3 s. m. and 3 pl. m. of all perfects are treated as in OJ (see OJ paradigm, p. 90).   Examples: הַקְרְבוּנִי, חַבְּלוּנִי, הַשְׁלְטָךְ, חַתְמַה.

The only examples of other parts of a perfect tense with suffixes are two of the 2 s. m. in Dan. 2. 23 (הֹודַעְתַּנִי and הֹודַעְתֶּנָא) and one 1 sing of a לא verb (note 5).

Imperf. stems.   3. Imperfects with suffixes closely resemble those of OJ and PTM (§ 36, note 8).   נַ. is combined with stems ending in a consonant and נ with stems ending in a vowel.   Exam-

ples : יְשַׁמְּשׁוּנֵּהּ, יְשֵׁיזְבִנְּךְ, יִתְּנֵנֵּהּ. With the suffix of the 2 pl. m. רְ is
written, without daghesh, and in one case the preceding vowel is
seghol (יְשֵׁיזְבִנְכוֹן, Dan. 3. 15; יִשְׁאֲלֶנְכוֹן, Ezra 7. 21). In the case
of two imperfects used in a jussive sense the suffixes are added to
the verbal stem without *nn* (יְבַהֲלָךְ, Dan. 4. 16; יְבַהֲלוּךְ, Dan. 5. 10).

Imperat. stems.   4. The only imperatt. with suffixes in OTA
are הַעֲלְנִי (Dan. 2. 24), חַבְּלוּהִי (Dan. 4. 20), and one from a ל״א
verb (note 5).   They agree with the forms of OJ (§ 36, note 9).

ל״א verbs.   5. There are seven cases in OTA of ל״א verbs
with suffixes attached.   The PERFECT form בֶּנַיְתַהּ ' I have built
it ' (Dan. 4. 27) is peculiar in having *ai* for *ē* (§ 28, note 6) and
seghol for vocal shewa.   Some MSS. read בְּנִיתַהּ.   The other cases
of perfect stems with suffixes (בְּנָהִי, שְׁנוֹהִי) agree with the practice
of OJ (§ 37, notes 2 and 5).

In the 3 s. m. IMPERFECT before ה the ṣere of the indepen-
dent form (יְחַוֵּה) is replaced by ḥireq (יְחַוֻּּה, יְחַוִּנַּי) and in the plural
ō is replaced by *u* (תְּהַחֲוֻנַּנִי, 2 pl. m. impf. Haphel).   For similar
forms in OJ see § 37, note 6.

The only ל״א IMPERATIVE form is the 2 pl. m. imperat.
Haphel הַחֲוֻנִי (Dan. 2. 6).

ע״י verbs.   6. No change takes place in the stems of ע״י verbs
when suffixes are attached (but see § 32, note 2).

PARADIGM OF VERB (OJ)

ITTAPHAL.	ITHPAAL.	ITHP^{e}EL.	APHEL.	PAEL.	P^{e}AL	P^{e}AL
			Perfects.			
אִתַּכְתַּב	אִתְכַּתַּב	אִתְכְּתִיב	אַכְתֵּיב	כַּתֵּיב	קְרֵיב	כְּתַב
אִתַּכְתְּבַת	אִתְכַּתְּבַת	אִתְכַּתִּיבַת	אַכְתֵּיבַת	כַּתֵּיבַת	קְרֵיבַת	כְּתַבַת
אִתַּכְתְּבַתָּא ־תְּ	אִתְכַּתַּבְתָּא ־תְּ	אִתְכַּתִּיבְתָּא ־תְּ	אַכְתֵּיבְתָּא ־תְּ	כַּתֵּיבְתָּא ־תְּ	קְרֵיבְתָּא ־תְּ	כְּתַבְתָּא ־תְּ
אִתַּכְתַּבְתְּ	אִתְכַּתַּבְתְּ	אִתְכַּתִּיבְתְּ	אַכְתֵּיבְתְּ	כַּתֵּיבְתְּ	קְרֵיבְתְּ	כְּתַבְתְּ
אִתַּכְתַּבִית	אִתְכַּתְּבִית	אִתְכַּתִּיבִית	אַכְתֵּיבִית	כַּתֵּיבִית	קְרֵיבִית	כְּתַבִית
אִתַּכְתַּבּוּ	אִתְכַּתַּבּוּ	אִתְכְּתִיבוּ	אַכְתִּיבוּ	כַּתֵּיבוּ	קְרֵיבוּ	כְּתַבוּ
אִתַּכְתַּבָא	אִתְכַּתְּבָא	אִתְכְּתִיבָא	אַכְתִּיבָא	כַּתֵּיבָא	קְרֵיבָא	כְּתַבָא
אִתַּכְתַּבְתּוּן	אִתְכַּתַּבְתּוּן	אִתְכַּתִּיבְתּוּן	אַכְתִּיבְתּוּן	כַּתֵּיבְתּוּן	קְרֵיבְתּוּן	כְּתַבְתּוּן
אִתַּכְתַּבְתִּין	אִתְכַּתַּבְתִּין	אִתְכַּתִּיבְתִּין	אַכְתֵּיבְתִּין	כַּתֵּיבְתִּין	קְרֵיבְתִּין	כְּתַבְתִּין
אִתַּכְתַּבְנָא	אִתְכַּתַּבְנָא	אִתְכַּתִּיבְנָא	אַכְתֵּיבְנָא	כַּתֵּיבְנָא	קְרֵיבְנָא	כְּתַבְנָא
			Imperfects.			
יִתַּכְתַּב	יִתְכַּתַּב	יִתְכְּתִיב	יַכְתֵּיב	יְכַתֵּיב	יִקְרַב	יִכְתּוֹב
תִּתַּכְתַּב	תִּתְכַּתַּב	תִּתְכְּתִיב	תַּכְתֵּיב	תְּכַתֵּיב	תִּקְרַב	תִּכְתּוֹב
תִּתַּכְתַּב	תִּתְכַּתַּב	תִּתְכְּתִיב	תַּכְתֵּיב	תְּכַתֵּיב	תִּקְרַב	תִּכְתּוֹב
תִּתַּכְתְּבִין	תִּתְכַּתְּבִין	תִּתְכַּתְּבִין	תַּכְתְּבִין	תְּכַתְּבִין	תִּקְרְבִין	תִּכְתְּבִין

	אִכְתּוֹב	אִקְרַב	אֱכַתֵּיב	אַכְתֵּיב	אִתְכְּתֵיב	אִתְכַּתַּב	אִתַּכְתַּב
	יִכְתְּבוּן	יִקְרְבוּן	יְכַתְּבוּן	יַכְתְּבוּן	יִתְכַּתְבוּן	יִתְכַּתְּבוּן	יִתַּכְתְּבוּן
	יִכְתְּבָן	יִקְרְבָן	יְכַתְּבָן	יַכְתְּבָן	יִתְכַּתְבָן	יִתְכַּתְּבָן	יִתַּכְתְּבָן
	תִּכְתְּבוּן	תִּקְרְבוּן	תְּכַתְּבוּן	תַּכְתְּבוּן	תִּתְכַּתְבוּן	תִּתְכַּתְּבוּן	תִּתַּכְתְּבוּן
	תִּכְתְּבָן	תִּקְרְבָן	תְּכַתְּבָן	תַּכְתְּבָן	תִּתְכַּתְבָן	תִּתְכַּתְּבָן	תִּתַּכְתְּבָן
	נִכְתּוֹב	נִקְרַב	נְכַתֵּיב	נַכְתֵּיב	נִתְכְּתֵיב	נִתְכַּתַּב	נִתַּכְתַּב

Imperatives.

כְּתוֹב	קְרַב	כַּתֵּיב	אַכְתֵּיב	אִתְכְּתֵיב	אִתְכַּתַּב	אִתַּכְתַּב
כְּתוּבִי	קְרַבִי	כַּתֵּיבִי	אַכְתֵּיבִי	אִתְכְּתֵיבִי	אִתְכַּתַּבִי	אִתַּכְתַּבִי
כְּתוּבוּ	קְרַבוּ	כַּתֵּיבוּ	אַכְתֵּיבוּ	אִתְכְּתֵיבוּ	אִתְכַּתַּבוּ	אִתַּכְתַּבוּ
כְּתוּבָא	קְרַבָא	כַּתֵּיבָא	אַכְתֵּיבָא	אִתְכְּתֵיבָא	אִתְכַּתַּבָא	אִתַּכְתַּבָא

Infinitives.

OJ	מִכְתַּב	מִקְרַב	כַּתָּבָא	אַכְתָּבָא	אִתְכְּתָבָא	אִתְכַּתָּבָא	אִתַּכְתָּבָא
PTM	מִכְתַּב, מִכְתּוֹב		מְכַתָּבָה	מַכְתָּבָה	מִתְכְּתָבָה	מִתְכַּתָּבָה	מִתַּכְתָּבָה

Participles.

כָּתֵיב	קָרֵיב	מְכַתֵּיב	מַכְתֵּיב	מִתְכְּתֵיב	מִתְכַּתַּב	מִתַּכְתַּב
כְּתִיב		מְכוּתַּב	מַכְתַּב			
		מְכַתַּב				

PARADIGM OF VERBAL SUFFIXES (OJ AND PTM)

Perfect.

	Pᴇᴀʟ.	PTM	Aᴘʜᴇʟ.	Pᴇᴀʟ.	PTM	Aᴘʜᴇʟ.
	3 sing. m		3 sing. m.	3 plur. m.		3 plur. m.

Imperfect.

	Pᴇᴀʟ.	PTM	Aᴘʜᴇʟ.
	3 sing. m.	PTM	3 plur. m.

יַרְדְּפוּנֵּיהּ		יִרְדְּפוּנֵּיהּ	יַרְדְּפִנֵּיהּ		יִרְדְּפִנֵּיהּ
יַרְדְּפוּנַּהּ		יִרְדְּפוּנַּהּ	יַרְדְּפִנַּהּ		יִרְדְּפִנַּהּ
יַרְדְּפוּנַּנָא	יִרְדְּפוּנַן	יִרְדְּפוּנַּנָא	יַרְדְּפִנַּנָא	יִרְדְּפִנַן	יִרְדְּפִנַּנָא
יַרְדְּפוּנְכוֹן		יִרְדְּפוּנְכוֹן	יַרְדְּפִנְכוֹן		יִרְדְּפִנְכוֹן
יַרְדִּיפוּנוּן	יִרְדְּפוּנוֹן	יִרְדְּפוּנְנוּן	יַרְדֵּיפִנּוּן	יִרְדְּפִנּוֹן	יִרְדְּפִנּוּן

Imperative.

2 plur. m.	PTM	2 plur. m.	2 sing. m.	PTM	2 sing. m.
אַרְדְּפוּנִי	רִדְפוּנִי	רִדְפוּנִי	אַרְדֵּיפְנִי	רִדְפִּי (רֵ׳)	רְדֹפְנִי
אַרְדְּפוּהִי	רִדְפוּנֵיהּ	רִדְפוּהִי	אַרְדֵּיפְהִי	רִדְפֵיהּ (רֵ׳)	רְדֹפְהִי
אַרְדְּפוּהָא	רִדְפוּנַהּ	רְדְפוּהָא	אַרְדֵּיפְהָא	רִדְפַהּ (רֵ׳)	רְדֹפְהָא
אַרְדְּפוּנָא	רִדְפוּנַן	רִדְפוּנָא	אַרְדֵּיפְנָא	רִדְפַן (רֵ׳)	רְדֹפְנָא
אַרְדִּיפוּנוּן	רִדְפוּנוֹן	רְדוּפוּנוּן	אַרְדֵּיפִנּוּן	רִדְפוֹן (רֵ׳)	רְדֹפִנּוּן

OLD TESTAMENT ARAMAIC

Personal pronouns (nominatives).

אֲנָה , אֲנָא	אֲנַ֫חְנָא	1 com.	
אַנְתְּ (אַנְתָּה)	אַנְתּוּן	2 masc.	
—	—	fem.	
הוּא , הֹם	3 masc.		
הִיא	הִמּוֹ	fem.	

Demonstrative pronouns and adjectives.

this	דֵּן	masc.	that	הוּא , דֵּךְ , דִּךְ
	דָּא	fem.		— , דֵּךְ , דָּךְ
these	אֵלֶּה , אִלֵּין		those	אִלֵּךְ
	(אֵלֶּה) אֵל			

Inflexion of Nouns.

Singular absolute.	יוֹם	מֶ֫לֶךְ
construct.	יוֹם	מֶ֫לֶךְ
emphatic.	יוֹמָא	מַלְכָּא

	Singular			Plural		
absolute.						
construct.						
emphatic.						

Nouns with suffixes.

	Singular.	Plural.		Singular.	Plural.
1 sing.					
2 s. m.					
f.					
3 s. m.					
f.					
1 plur.					
2 pl. m.					
f.					
3 pl. m.					
f.					

94

OTA PARADIGM OF VERB

	HOPHAL.	HITHPAAL.	HITHPᵉEL.	HAPHEL.	HAPHEL.	PAEL.	PᵉAL.	PᵉAL.	
									Perfect.
כְּתַב	הָכְתַּב	הִתְכַּתַּב	הִתְכְּתֵב	הַכְתֵּב	הַכְתֵּב	כַּתֵּב[1]	כְּתִיב[1]	כְּתַב	3 s. m.
	הָכְתְּבַה		הִתְכַּתְּבַת				הָכְתְּבַת	כְּתַבַת	f.
		הִתְכַּתַּבְתְּ	הִתְכְּתֵבְתְּ	הַכְתֵּבְתְּ			כְּתַבְתְּ	כְּתַבְתְּ	2 s. m.
			הִ-	הִ-			הִ-	הִ-	f.
		הִתְכַּתְּבֵת	הִתְכְּתֵבֵת	הַכְתְּבֵת		כַּתְּבֵת	כִּתְבֵת	כִּתְבֵת	1 sing.
		הִתְכַּתַּבוּ	הִתְכְּתֵבוּ			כַּתִּבוּ	כְּתִבוּ	כְּתַבוּ	3 pl. m.
								כְּתַבָא	f.
		הִתְכַּתַּבְתּוּן	הִתְכְּתֵבְתּוּן					כְּתַבְתּוּן	2 pl. m.
									f.
		הִתְכַּתַּבְנָא	הִתְכְּתֵבְנָא	הַכְתֵּבְנָא			הִכְתְּבְנָא	כְּתַבְנָא	1 pl.
									Imperfect.
	יִתְכַּתַּב	יִתְכְּתֵב[1]	יְהַכְתֵּב[1]	יְהַכְתֵּב	(יְקַטֵּל)[1]	יִכְתֵּב	יִכְתֻּב	3 s. m.
	תִּתְכַּתַּב	תִּתְכְּתֵב	תְּהַכְתֵּב	תְּהַכְתֵּב		תִּכְתֵּב	תִּכְתֻּב	f.

2 s. m.						
f.						
1 sing.[2]						
3 pl. m.						
f.						
2 pl. m.						
f.						
1 pl.						
Imperative.						
2 s. m.						
f.						
2 pl. m.						
Infinitive.						
Ptc. act.						
Ptc. pass.						

[1] See § 16, note 12.   [2] See § 18, notes 3 and 4

OLD TESTAMENT ARAMAIC

TABLE OF VERBS

	ע״ע	ע״ו	ל״א	פ״י	ל״ה	א״פ	פ״נ		
פְּעַל									
עַל	קָם	מְטָא	יְדַע	הֲוָה	אֲמַר	נְפַק	כְּתַב		Perf.
(יֵעֹל)	(יְקוּם)	יִמְטֵא	יִנְדַּע		יֵאמַר	[יִפֻּק]	יִכְתֻּב		Imperf.
	קוּם		דַּע	הֱוֵי	אֱמַר	פֻּק	כְּתֻב		Imperat.
(מֵעַל)	(מְקָם)				מֵאמַר	[מִפַּק]	מִכְתַּב		Infin.
					אָמַר		כָּתֵב		Ptc. act.
						נְפִיק	כְּתִיב		Ptc. pass.
הַפְעֵל									
הַנְעֵל	הֲקֵים		הוֹדַע				הַכְתֵּב		Perf.
יְהַנְעֵל	יְהָקֵים		יְהוֹדַע				יְהַכְתֵּב		Imperf.
הַנְעֵל	הֲקֵים						הַכְתֵּב		Imperat.
הַנְעָלָה	הֲקָמָה		הוֹדָעָה	הַחֲוָיָה		הַנְפָּקָה	הַכְתָּבָה		Infin.
(מְהַנְעֵל)	(מְהָקֵים)				אָזֵל		מְהַכְתֵּב		Ptc. act.
	הֲקַם						מְהַכְתַּב		Ptc. pass.

APPENDIX ON THE NUMERALS[1]

by J. A. EMERTON

Introduction

WHEN the late Dr. W. B. Stevenson compiled this grammar, he apparently accepted Dalman's views about the Aramaic dialects of Palestine. Dalman believed that the best evidence for the Aramaic spoken in Palestine in the early centuries of our era was to be found in the Targums of Onkelos and Jonathan, and in the Palestinian Talmud and Midrashim. He thought that the Jerusalem Targums were later in date and of much less value.

Dalman's views have been challenged in more recent years, notably by P. E. Kahle.[2] Largely as a result of his work on fragments of the Targums of Onkelos and Jonathan with Babylonian pointing, and on fragments of the Palestinian Targum, he argues that the former Targums were produced in Babylonia in an artificial literary Aramaic, and that they are not good evidence for the language spoken in Palestine. On the other hand, he believes that the Jerusalem Targums contain material derived from the older Palestinian Targum. This Palestinian Targum (which is not to be regarded as a single, uniform translation) reflects the spoken Palestinian language. Since Kahle published fragments of this version, A. Diez Macho has discovered the Palestinian Targum to the whole Pentateuch in a Vatican manuscript.[3]

Kahle's conclusions have not been universally accepted.

---

[1] I am indebted to Professor G. R. Driver, Professor D. Winton Thomas, and the Rev. A. E. Goodman for their kindness in reading the first draft of the first few pages of this appendix.

[2] *The Cairo Geniza* (2nd edn., Oxford, 1959), pp. 191–208.

[3] Cf. *Congress Volume, Oxford 1959* (Supplements to Vetus Testamentum, vii) (Leiden, 1960), pp. 222 ff.

E. Y. Kutscher, for example, has recently[1] maintained that the Targum of Onkelos has an ultimately Palestinian origin, even though it does not reflect ordinary spoken usage. Nevertheless, it cannot be denied that Dalman's views are now out of date. The Palestinian Targum ought now to be used in the preparation of a grammar of Palestinian Jewish Aramaic, and it is, at least, questionable whether the language of the Targums of Onkelos and Jonathan should be included.

If, therefore, Stevenson were preparing this *Grammar of Palestinian Jewish Aramaic* today, it is likely that he would make a different selection of dialects. Nevertheless, although its contents no longer adequately represent modern knowledge of Palestinian Aramaic, his work retains its usefulness as a description of the dialects with which it deals. This appendix describes the numerals in OJ and PTM, so as to add to the usefulness of the book without altering its scope.

Similarly, I have adopted Stevenson's policy of transliterating supralinear punctuation into the more familiar sublinear system.[2] This policy is sometimes unsatisfactory, but it seems desirable that the appendix should be uniform with the rest of the book. I have also brought the spelling of some words into line with Stevenson's methods of orthography. Consonantal waw and yodh, for example, are shown by single, not double, letters.[3] This procedure is justified by the fact that this book is intended primarily for fairly elementary students. For the same reason, I have simplified other matters. For instance, some fairly rare forms have been omitted, and no attempt has been made to record all the varieties of punctuation or of the consonantal text which are found in the manuscripts and editions.[4]

It will be obvious to many readers that this treatment of the

---

[1] C. Rabin and Y. Yadin, *Scripta Hierosolymitana*, iv (Jerusalem, 1958), pp. 9 f.   [2] Cf. pp. 3, 11 ff.   [3] Cf. p. 11.

[4] I have usually been guided by Sperber's edition of the Targum and by Dalman's *Aramäisch-neuhebräisches Handwörterbuch zu Targum, Talmud, und Midrasch* (Göttingen, 1938 edn.), as well as by Dalman's grammar.

numerals is greatly indebted to G. Dalman's *Grammatik des jüdisch-palästinischen Aramäisch* (2nd edn., Leipzig, 1905) and draws on the material which he has collected. I have also been able to use several works which have appeared since Stevenson wrote, including H. Odeberg's *The Aramaic Portions of Bereshit Rabba with Grammar of Galilaean Aramaic* (Lund, 1939) and J. F. Stenning's *The Targum of Isaiah* (Oxford, 1949).

In 1959 Alexander Sperber published the first two volumes of *The Bible in Aramaic* (Leiden), containing the Targums of Onkelos on the Pentateuch and of Jonathan on the Former Prophets. A future volume will contain the text of the Latter Prophets, and the final volume will give a full introduction to the edition. Until this last volume is published, it will not be possible fully to evaluate Sperber's work, but there can be no doubt of the importance and usefulness of an edition based on so many manuscripts and printed texts. I have made extensive use of the first two volumes in the preparation of this appendix.

For Old Testament Aramaic, I have used *Grammatik des Biblisch-Aramäischen* (Halle, 1927) by H. Bauer and P. Leander. The references to the Aramaic of Daniel and Ezra are taken from the text in the third edition of Rudolf Kittel's *Biblia Hebraica* (Stuttgart, 1937).

THE NUMERALS

Note. There are many variations in spelling in the manuscripts and printed editions. In particular, most forms which are shown below as ending in א or ה also appear with ה or א respectively as the final letter. Similarly, 'ten' and related numbers frequently have ט instead of ס.

§ 39. CARDINAL NUMBERS

OJ. 1. Cardinal numbers 1–19

	With masculine nouns	*With feminine nouns*
1	חַד	חֲדָא

	With masculine nouns	*With feminine nouns*
2	תְּרֵין, תְּרֵי	תַּרְתֵּין
3	תְּלָתָה	תְּלָת
4	אַרְבְּעָה (construct אַרְבְּעַת)	אַרְבַּע
5	חַמְשָׁה (¹חֲמֵשַׁת construct)	חֲמֵשׁ
6	שִׁתָּה (construct שִׁתַּת)	שִׁית
7	שִׁבְעָה (construct שִׁבְעַת)	שְׁבַע
8	תְּמַנְיָא	תַּמְנֵי, תְּמָנֵי, תְּמָנָא
9	תִּשְׁעָה (construct תִּשְׁעַת)	תְּשַׁע, תִּישַׁע, תִּישְׁעַ
10	עַסְרָה	עֲסַר
11	חַד עֲסַר	חֲדָא עֶסְרֵי, חֲדָא עֶ׳
12	תְּרֵין עֲסַר, תְּרֵי עֶ׳	תַּרְתָּא עֶסְרֵי, תַּרְתֵּין עֶ׳, תַּרְתֵּי עֶ׳
13	תְּלָת עֲסַר	תְּלָת עֶסְרֵי
14	אַרְבְּעַת עֲסַר	אַרְבַּע עֶסְרֵי
15	¹חֲמֵשַׁת עֲסַר	חֲמֵשׁ עֶסְרֵי
16	שִׁתַּת עֲסַר	שִׁית עֶסְרֵי
17	²שִׁבְעַת עֲסַר	שְׁבַע עֶסְרֵי
18	תְּמָנַת עֲסַר	תַּמְנֵי עֶסְרֵי, תְּמָנָא עֶ׳, תַּמְנָא עֶ׳
19	תִּשְׁעַת עֲסַר	תְּשַׁע עֶסְרֵי, תִּישַׁע עֶ׳

Such forms as the following are also found with masculine
nouns: שִׁית עֶ׳, חֲמֵשׁ עֶ׳, חַמְשָׁא עֶ׳, אַרְבְּעָה עֶ׳, תְּלָתָא עֲסַר.

PTM. 2

PTM use the same forms as OJ for the units, with the addition
of the following variants:

	With masculine nouns	*With feminine nouns*
2	תְּרֵין, תְּרֵי	תַּרְתֵּי, תַּרְתֵּי
6	אַשְׁתָּה, אַשְׁתָּה	
7	³שׁובעה	
8	³תומניא	

[1] Sometimes vocalized חֲמִישְׁתְּ.

[2] I can find no example of this form in OJ, but this is presumably what it
should be.

[3] Note the tendency for the vowel to become *u* before the labials beth
and mem.

PTM. 3

PTM differ from OJ in the numerals 10–19 in the following
ways:

(a) עֲשָׂרָה is frequently used instead of עֶסְרֵי.

(b) Sometimes, worn-away forms (cf. the Babylonian Talmud
and the Jerusalem Targums) are used, in which the ע of
עסר has been lost, e.g.

    11 (with masculine noun) חַדְסַר

    12 (with feminine noun) תְּרֵיסְרֵי

    16 (with masculine noun) אשית תיסר

(c) There are minor differences, e.g. (with masculine noun)
תשעה ע׳, תמני ע׳, שבעה ע׳, שובעת עשר[1], שובעה.

OJ and PTM. 4. Tens

20	עֶסְרִין	30	תְּלָתִין	40	אַרְבְּעֵין
50	חַמְשִׁין	60	שִׁתִּין	70	שִׁבְעִין
80	תַּמְנָן, תְּמָנִין	90	תִּשְׁעִין		

PTM also have אֶשְׁתִּין, אֶשְׁתִּין for 60, שׁוּבְעִין[1] for 70, and תּוּמְנִין[1]
for 80.

OJ and PTM. 5. Hundreds

The word for 'hundred' is מְאָה.

OJ use the following forms:

200	מָאתַן, מָתַן	300	תְּלָת מְאָה
400	אַרְבַּע מְאָה	500	חֲמֵישׁ מְאָה
600	שֵׁית מְאָה·	700	שְׁבַע מְאָה
800	תַּמְנֵי מְאָה	900	תְּשַׁע מְאָה

PTM sometimes use the same forms, but also have מָאתַיִן for 200,
and, for 300–900, more frequently have מָאוָן (the absolute plural
of מְאָה) preceded by the short form of the numeral, e.g. תלת
מאון (also תשעת מאון, ארבע מאון, תשע מאון).

---

[1] Note the tendency for the vowel to become *u* before the labials beth
and mem.

OJ and PTM. 6. Thousands

In both OJ and PTM, the word for 'thousand' is אֲלַף, emphatic state אַלְפָּא; plural: absolute אַלְפִין, emphatic אַלְפַיָּא.

OJ and PTM use the plural of אלף, preceded by the form of the numeral appropriate to a masculine noun, e.g. 2,000 תְּרֵין אַלְפִין; 3,000 תְּלָתָה אַלְפִין; 14,000 אַרְבְּעַת עֲסַר אַלְפִין.

OJ and PTM. 7. Myriads

Tens of thousands can be expressed as in note 6 above, e.g. 20,000 עֶסְרִין אַלְפִין; 200,000 מָאתַן אַלְפִין.

Sometimes, however, the word for 'myriad' is used: absolute state רִבּוֹ, emphatic רִבּוֹתָא; plural: absolute רִבְוָן, emphatic רִבְוָתָא or רִבָּנְתָא, construct רִבְּוַת. As the noun is feminine, any other numerals preceding it take the form appropriate to this gender, e.g. 1 Kings 8. 63 תַּרְתֵּין רִבּוֹ ... תַּרְתֵּין רִבּוֹ עֶסְרֵי רִבּוֹ.

OJ and PTM. 8. Compound numerals

The higher numbers come first, and the lower numbers are joined by וְ, e.g.

Gen. 5. 26 שְׁבַע מְאָה וּתְמָנַן וְתַרְתֵּין שְׁנִין 782 years.
Num. 26. 22 שִׁבְעִין וְשִׁתָּה אַלְפִין וַחֲמֵשׁ מְאָה 76,500.

PTM. 9

The numerals 3–10 and 20–90 also have a determinate form ending in *tē*, e.g. תְּלָתֵי 'the three'; אַרְבַּעְתֵּי 'the four'; חַמְשֵׁתֵּי 'the five'; תּוּמַנְתֵּי 'the eight'; תְּלָת עֶשְׂרֵתֵּי 'the thirteen'; תְּלָתֵיתֵי 'the thirty'.

OJ and PTM. 10. Special forms for the days of the week or month

In PTM, special forms (ending in *ā* or *tā*) are used for the days of the week: Monday תְּרֵיָא; Tuesday תְּלָתָא; Wednesday אַרְבַּעְתָּא; Thursday חַמְשְׁתָּא.

In OJ, the numbers 10–19, when referring to a day of the month, have the emphatic form עַסְרָא, e.g.

Exod. 12. 3 בְּעַסְרָא לְיַרְחָא 'on the tenth of the month'.

Josh. 5. 10 בְּאַרְבְּעַת עַסְרָא יוֹמָא לְיַרְחָא 'on the fourteenth day of the month'.

OJ and PTM. 11. Suffixes

In PTM, suffixes can be attached to the numerals 2–9, though examples of some of the possible forms are lacking.

2 feminine תַּרְתֵּיהוֹן; תַּרְוַיְהוֹן, תַּרְוַיְהוֹן, תְּרֵיכוֹן

3 תלתיהון

8 תמניתהון, ¹תמנותיהון

Similar forms appear in OJ, e.g. שִׁבְעָתְהוֹן, תְּלָתֵּיכוֹן. Before suffixes, the form corresponding to תְּרֵין is תַּרְוֵי, e.g. תַּרְוֵיהוֹן.

OTA. 12

The following forms are found in OTA:

	With masculine nouns		With feminine nouns
1	חַד		חֲדָא, חֲדָה
2	——		תַּרְתֵּין
3	תְּלָתָא, תְּלָתָה		תְּלָת
4	אַרְבְּעָה		אַרְבַּע
6	——		שֵׁת, שָׁת
7	שִׁבְעָה (construct שִׁבְעַת)		——
10	עַשְׂרָה		עֲשַׂר
12	תְּרֵי־עֲשַׂר		——

20	עֶשְׂרִין	30	תְּלָתִין	60	שִׁתִּין
100	מְאָה	200	מָאתַיִן	400	אַרְבַּע מְאָה

1000 אֲלַף, construct אֲלָף, emphatic אַלְפָּא; plural: absolute אֲלָפִין,² emphatic אַלְפַיָּא.

10,000 construct singular רִבּוֹ;

absolute plural רבון (Kᵉthibh; Qᵉre רִבְבָן).

---

¹ Dalman emends this form to תמניתיהון.

² The reading אלפים in Dan. 7. 10 is probably a mistake.

With a suffix תְּלָתֵּהוֹן.

In the only two examples of compound numerals, the lower number follows the higher and is linked to it by וְ:

62. שִׁתִּין וְתַרְתֵּין   Dan. 6. 1

120. מְאָה וְעֶשְׂרִין   Dan. 6. 2

§ 40. ORDINAL NUMBERS

OJ and PTM. 1. 'First'

The word for 'first' is קַדְמַי (or קַדְמָאי; cf. p. 28), emphatic state קַדְמָאָה; plural: absolute קַדְמָאִין, emphatic קַדְמָאֵי; feminine singular emphatic קַדְמָיתָא, plural emphatic קַדְמָיתָא.

קַדְמַי is attached to the F class of nouns (cf. pp. 28–37), and variations in form occur, similar to those of עִבְרָי, e.g. masculine singular emphatic קַדְמָיָא, masculine plural absolute קַדְמָיִין. PTM also have a form in which the daleth has coalesced with the mem, which is doubled in compensation: קַמַּי, &c. (also קוּמָיא).

OJ and PTM. 2. 'Second'

The word for 'second' is תִּנְיָן, emphatic תִּנְיָנָא; plural absolute תִּנְיָנִין; feminine singular absolute תִּנְיֵיתָא, &c.

OJ and PTM. 3. 'Third'–'tenth'

The following forms, declined like F nouns, are used:

3rd תְּלִיתִי	4th רְבִיעִי	5th חֲמִישׁ	6th שְׁתִיתִי
7th שְׁבִיעִי	8th תְּמִינִי	9th תְּשִׁיעִי	10th עֲסִירִי

The feminine singular emphatic is תְּלִיתִיתָא, רְבִיעִיתָא, &c.

OJ and PTM. 4

The cardinal numerals serve as ordinals for higher numbers.

OTA. 5

OTA has the following forms:

'First': masculine plural emphatic קַדְמָיָא
            feminine singular emphatic קַדְמָיְתָא, plural emphatic
            קַדְמָיָתָא

'Second': feminine singular absolute תִּנְיָנָה

'Third': feminine singular absolute תְּלִיתָאָה (Qᵉre; Kᵉthibh
          תליתיא)

'Fourth': masculine singular emphatic רְבִיעָאָה (Qᵉre; Kᵉthibh
          רביעיא)
          feminine singular absolute רְבִיעָאָה (Qᵉre; Kᵉthibh
          רביעיה and רביעיא)
          feminine singular emphatic רְבִיעָיְתָא

The forms תַּלְתָּא and תַּלְתִּי in Dan. 5. 7, 16, 29 are used of an
important office in the Babylonian kingdom. They seem to be
loan-words from Akkadian, and are not to be regarded as Aramaic numerals. Cf. J. A. Montgomery, *A Critical and Exegetical
Commentary on the Book of Daniel* (Edinburgh, 1927), pp. 256 f.

§ 41. OTHER NUMERALS

Note. Some of these forms are very rare. For convenience,
OJ and PTM are usually grouped together in this section, but
this does not mean that all the forms mentioned are found in both
dialects.

1. Distributives

These are expressed by repetition of the cardinal numeral, e.g.
Num. 3. 47 חֲמֵשׁ חֲמֵשׁ סִלְעִין 'five shekels each'.
Sometimes, the numbered object is also repeated, e.g.
Isa. 6. 2 שִׁתָּא גַפִּין שִׁתָּא גַפִּין לְחַד 'each one had six wings'.

2. Ordinal adverbs

These are expressed by the masculine ordinal numeral in the
absolute state, by the feminine ordinal numeral in the emphatic
state with the preposition בְּ, and, in the case of certain numbers,
by a form ending in *ā̆(th)*, e.g.

'First' קַדְמִי, בְּקַדְמֵיתָא, קַדְמוּתָא (Isa. 60. 9 אִידָא פָּרְסָא קלְעָהָא
בְּקַדְמֵיתָא 'Which spreads out its sails first?')
'Second' בְּתִנְיֵיתָא; 'third' תְּלִיתַי, בְּתְלִיתִיתָא, &c.

The same forms are used to express the meaning 'the first time', 'the second time', &c. Note the form תִּנְיָנוּת, תִּנְיָנוּ[1] 'the second time'. It is also possible to use a cardinal numeral with זְמַן (cf. note 3 (a) below).

3. Multiplicatives

(a) The question 'How often?' is answered by the cardinal numeral with זְמַן, זִמְנָא, or זִמְנִין (treated sometimes as masculine and sometimes as feminine), e.g. זִמְנָא חֲדָא (or חַד זְמַן) 'once'; שְׁבַע זִמְנִין 'seven times'; תִּשְׁעָה זִמְנִין 'nine times'. Sometimes, חֲדָא is used alone, e.g. חֲדָא בְּשַׁתָּא 'once a year'.

In OTA (Dan. 6. 11, 14) the numeral follows זִמְנִין: זִמְנִין תְּלָתָה 'three times'.

Multiplication is expressed in PTM by the use of cardinal numerals, often with זִמְנִין and the preposition מִן, e.g. חַמְשִׁין זִמְנִין מִן מְאָה 50×100. When a number is squared, the preposition עַל may be used, e.g. חַמְשִׁין עַל חַמְשִׁין 50×50.

(b) The meaning 'threefold', 'fourfold', &c., is expressed by the phrase עַל חַד followed by the appropriate numeral, e.g.

Gen. 26. 12 וַיִּשְׁכַּח בְּשַׁתָּא הַהִיא עַל חַד מְאָה 'and he found an hundredfold in that year'.

2 Sam. 12. 6 יְשַׁלֵּם עַל חַד אַרְבָּעָא 'he shall repay fourfold'.

In OTA, a slightly different construction is used in Dan. 3. 19 לְמֵזֵא לְאַתּוּנָא חַד־שִׁבְעָה עַל דִּי חֲזֵה לְמֵזְיַהּ 'to heat the furnace seven times hotter than it was usual to heat it'.

4. Fractions

There are two ways of expressing fractions:

(a) By the use of cardinal numerals and the preposition לְ or מִן, e.g. חֲדָא לַעֲשַׂר 1/10; חַד מִן עַסְרָא 1/10; חַד מִן שִׁתָּא 1/6; חַד מִן עֲשַׂר 1/10.

(b) By the use of special forms:

(i) 'A half': פְּלַג or פְּלִיג;[2] emphatic state פַּלְגָּא or פַּלְגָּא.

---

[1] Found also in OTA (Dan. 2. 7).

[2] OTA has פְּלַג (construct—Dan. 7. 25); פְּלִיג resembles the Syriac ܦܠܓ. Other variants are also found in the manuscripts.

In addition to this form, which belongs to the A class of nouns, there is a form belonging to the G class: פְּלֵג, construct פַּלְגוּת, &c., e.g.

Exod. 37. 6 תַּרְתֵּין אַמִּין וּפַלְגָּא '2½ cubits'.

Num. 34. 15 תְּרֵין שִׁבְטִין וּפַלְגוּת שִׁבְטָא 'the two tribes and the half tribe'.

(ii) Other forms:

1/3 תַּלְתּוּת, also תַּלְתָּא, תִּלְתָּא, תְּלָתָא

1/4 רְבִיַע, emphatic רְבִיעָא and רַבְעָא; construct רַבְעוּת and רִבְעַת; plural רָבְעִין, &c.

1/5 חוֹמֶשׁ, חֻמְשָׁא

1/6 שְׁתּוּת

1/7 שׁוֹבַע, שְׁבְעָא

1/8 תְּמָנְתָא, תַּמְנְתָא[1]

1/10 עִסּוּר; מַעַסְרָא 'tithe'; עֶסְרוֹנָא '1/10 of an ephah'

---

[1] Cf. Odeberg's note on the vocalization of these two forms.

PRINTED IN GREAT BRITAIN
AT THE UNIVERSITY PRESS, OXFORD
BY VIVIAN RIDLER
PRINTER TO THE UNIVERSITY